Microwaving One-Dish Dinners

MICROWAVE
COOKING
INSTITUTE

Prentice Hall Press • New York

microwave cooking library®

By conventional standards, any dish cooked in a microwave oven is fast. Microwave oven owners expect speed with microwave cooking; when they ask for fast-cooking main dishes, they mean *really* fast.

Microwaving One-Dish Dinners explores several approaches to meeting that goal. It provides recipes for a variety of occasions and life styles. Whether you choose a family favorite, a make-ahead main dish, or a special company presentation, you'll find recipes that minimize preparation time and effort while they take full advantage of microwave speed.

In addition to recipes, the book offers timesaving ideas for weekly menu planning, marketing and organizing the pantry and freezer efficiently. Look for the tinted boxes that accompany each recipe. They include fast and easy accomplishments to complete the meal. With this book you'll discover how fast and easy microwave cooking can be.

Barbara Methven
Barbara Methven

CREDITS:
Design & Production: Cy DeCosse Incorporated
Senior Art Director: Bill Nelson
Art Director: Rebecca Gammelgaard
Managing Editor: Reneé Dignan
Editorial Assistant: Sally Stickel
Home Economists: Jill Crum, Peggy Ramette, Kathy Weber, Grace Wells, Sandy Engen
Recipe Editor: Myrna Shaw
Production Consultant: Christine Watkins
Production Manager: Jim Bindas
Assistant Production Manager: Julie Churchill
Typesetting: Jennie Smith, Linda Schloegel, Bryan Trandem
Production Staff: Janice Cauley, Barb Falk, Michele Joy, Yelena Konrardy, Carol McMall, Lisa Rosenthal, David Schelitzche, Cathleen Shannon, Nik Wogstad
Photographers: Tony Kubat, John Lauenstein, Mette Nielsen, Rex Irmen
Food Stylists: Teresa Ernst, Susan Sinon, Lynn Bachman, Suzanne Finley, Carol Grones, Robin Krause, Lynn Lohmann, Susan Zechmann
Color Separations: Weston Engraving Co., Inc.
Printing: R. R. Donnelley & Sons (0387)

Additional volumes in the Microwave Cooking Library series are available from the publisher:
· Basic Microwaving
· Microwaving Meats
· Microwaving Meals in 30 Minutes
· Microwaving on a Diet
· 101 Microwaving Secrets
· Microwaving Light & Healthy
· Microwaving Poultry & Seafood
· The Joy of Microwaving
· Country Kitchen Microwaving

CY DE COSSE INCORPORATED
Chairman: Cy DeCosse
President: James B. Maus
Executive Vice President: William B. Jones

Copyright © 1987 by Cy DeCosse Incorporated
5900 Green Oak Drive
Minnetonka, Minnesota 55343
All rights reserved, including the right of reproduction in whole or in part in any form.

Library of Congress Cataloging-in-Publication Data.
Methven, Barbara.
  Microwaving one-dish dinners.

  (Microwave cooking library)
  Originally published under title: Microwaving fast & easy main dishes.
  Includes index.
  1. Microwave cookery. 2. Cookery (Entrées)
I. Microwave Cooking Institute. II. Title.
III. Series: Methven, Barbara. Microwave cooking library.
TX832.M39675 1987b 641.5'882 87-43027
ISBN 0-13-183799-0

Published by Prentice Hall Press
A Division of Simon & Schuster, Inc.
Gulf+Western Building
One Gulf+Western Plaza
New York, NY 10023
PRENTICE HALL PRESS is a trademark of Simon & Schuster, Inc.
Manufactured in the United States of America
10 9 8 7 6 5 4 3 2 1
First Edition

Contents

What You Need to Know Before You Start 5
How to Use This Book.. 6
What to Keep On Hand In Your Pantry 8
Refrigerator Management................................. 10
About Reheating.. 11
Fast & Easy From the Freezer 12
Freezer Packaging 14
About Defrosting... 15
Family Favorites 19
    Beef.. 21
    Pork.. 39
    Poultry... 49
    Fish & Seafood 69
    Meatless.. 81
Company Fare 87
    Beef.. 89
    Pork.. 93
    Lamb.. 97
    Veal... 98
    Poultry... 101
    Fish & Seafood 109
Light & Easy... 115
    Beef.. 117
    Pork.. 122
    Poultry... 125
    Fish & Seafood 133
Make-Ahead 141

What You Need to Know Before You Start

A microwave oven has many advantages, but the most popular one is speed. In the growing number of households in which all the members are either at work or in school, the microwave oven is becoming a basic appliance. Whoever prepares the food must do it at the end of a busy day. Microwave cooking is fast. It can be even faster when you know how to take full advantage of its speed and convenience.

Save Time Before You Cook

The first way to save time in food preparation is to know what you are going to cook and have all the ingredients necessary for preparation. In the long run, it will save time if you devote some time each week to planning the week's menus.

Take your cookbook and some scratch paper to a quiet spot. Put your feet up. Here's your chance to page through the book, noting recipes you want to try or foods you can cook once and serve twice. Check the supermarket ads for good buys, so you can plan in advance what you'll do with the specials.

Take a moment to check your refrigerator, freezer and pantry for ingredients you already have on hand. Then, make a complete list of everything you will need to buy in order to prepare the meals you've planned. Don't forget seasonings and staples. The fifteen minutes needed to microwave a main dish can stretch to an hour or more when you have to drop everything and run out and purchase a forgotten ingredient.

Every recipe in this book includes suggestions for foods to complete the meal. These foods can be prepared from scratch or from boxed mixes the night before, or purchased at the delicatessen, bakery or frozen foods cases of the supermarket. If you like the suggestions, add those foods to your shopping list, too.

Save Time As You Cook

Microwaving time is only part of total cooking time. Preparation counts as well. The recipes in this book have been designed to shorten preparation time. Chopping and slicing are kept to a minimum. The number of ingredients is limited. Even the longest recipes have only ten ingredients, plus seasonings.

Limiting the number of ingredients doesn't mean limiting flavor. The recipes make creative use of the newest convenience foods, such as pre-chopped fresh or frozen vegetable combinations, seasoned rices and seasoning mixes. Added to your fresh ingredients, these packaged foods contribute flavor and save preparation time.

Time saving shouldn't mean sacrificing family favorites, like turkey or ribs. This book provides recipes for longer-cooking foods which can be microwaved in an hour or less. Any preparation is done the day before, so the food is ready to place in the microwave oven without additional preparation at meal time.

Another way to save time is to make efficient use of your freezer and refrigerator for foods which are fully prepared and ready to heat. The microwave oven reheats foods to just-cooked flavor, texture and temperature.

For some menus, a combination of microwave and conventional cooking provides the fastest food preparation. Microwave a sauce while the pasta cooks conventionally, or microwave the filling while the tortillas soften conventionally.

How to Use This Book

This book provides tasty, easy to prepare and fast cooking main dishes. Many recipes include reheating directions so an on-the-go family can use single servings as needed. The different sections reflect a variety of situations for which you might want recipes.

Lemony Fillets & Rice		
Green Beans	Whole Wheat Muffins	Cheesecake

The tinted box accompanying each main dish recipe suggests menus which were chosen with regard to taste, color, texture and temperature.

Family Favorites. Recipes in this section are economical and traditional favorites, updated to take advantage of the latest convenience foods. They make four to six servings and appeal to children as well as adults. The dishes are down-home, but definitely not dull. Seasonings are flavorful and familiar rather than exotic. If your family prefers food hot and spicy, add a little more seasoning to taste.

Company Fare. While not extravagant, these special occasion main dishes are a little more costly than everyday recipes. They demonstrate that it's possible to produce an elegant meal in a limited time. Some of the recipes serve eight people, while others are for more intimate dinners.

Light & Easy. These main dishes reflect the growing tendency toward lighter meals. They are suitable for hot summer days, Sunday suppers or luncheons. Besides sandwiches and soups, there are hot main dish salads and light entrees.

Make-Ahead. There are two ways you can save time and effort during the meal-time rush by cooking ahead at a time which is more leisurely and convenient for you. Some main dishes can be frozen in single portions for use by family members who can't be home at mealtime. Consider these when you leave the children with a baby sitter. Plan ahead for an extra-busy day by preparing one of the recipes which make two batches of family-size main dishes. Serve one immediately and freeze the other. The recipes include directions for taking the second batch from freezer to table for serving. Another time saver is the make-ahead mix. Batches of meat sauce, vegetable sauce or meatballs can be divided into several recipe-size portions and frozen. When combined with other ingredients, they produce several totally different main dishes.

What to Keep on Hand In Your Pantry

The well-stocked pantry, refrigerator and freezer can save you both time and money. Buy frequently used items in quantity when they are supermarket specials. If you stock up on canned goods periodically, you can skip those aisles on busy shopping days. To spread out the cost of stocking up, add to your soup supply one week, pasta and rice the next and canned meat and fish on a third. Modern cooks are not content to use convenience foods only for the dishes provided in the package directions. Many convenience foods can be turned into staple ingredients for totally different dishes. Include them in your basic food stock, too.

Keep Supplies Up-to-date

As you use an item, put it on your next shopping list. If you follow the week-by-week method of supply, inventory a small section of your pantry or freezer weekly. Perhaps you need to buy several packages of frequently used items, or plan to use up something you've had on hand for awhile. Remember to keep spices and condiments current, too. These items often take you by surprise when they run out just as you need them.

Be Ready for Emergencies

On those occasions when you haven't had time to shop in advance, your pantry and freezer can save you a last-minute trip to the supermarket. Keep a supply of ingredients for those emergency main dishes and replace items as they are used so you'll be ready next time. As you try the recipes in this book, take note of those you could whip up from on-hand ingredients. Even with the best of intentions, most shoppers yield to impulse buying occasionally. When you bring home that terrific unplanned bargain, a well-stocked pantry can supply what you need to make use of it.

Make Substitutions

No matter how well you plan, there will be times when a necessary ingredient didn't make it onto the shopping list. Your pantry, refrigerator or freezer may yield a good substitute. Perhaps you would like to try a recipe in this book, but one ingredient doesn't suit your family's taste. The following chart suggests some substitutions and equivalent measurements.

How to Make Substitutions

Ingredient:	Substitution:
1 lb. ground beef	1 lb. ground turkey
2 cups cut-up cooked chicken	2 cups cut-up cooked turkey, or 2 cans chunk chicken
2 cups fully cooked ham	2 cups cubed turkey ham
1 can chunk chicken	1 can chunk ham
1 can tuna	1 can salmon
1 cup ready-to-serve chicken or beef broth	1 cup hot water plus 1 teaspoon (chicken or beef) instant bouillon granules
1 cup whole milk	½ cup evaporated milk plus ½ cup water
1 tablespoon cornstarch	2 tablespoons all-purpose flour
Fresh garlic clove	Equivalent amount of garlic powder, or instant minced garlic
Fresh chopped onion	Equivalent amount of instant minced onion
Fresh snipped parsley	⅓ to ½ amount of dried parsley flakes

How to Stock the Pantry

Canned or Bottled Foods

Beans (Garbanzo, Great Northern, Kidney, Refried)
Broth (Beef & Chicken)
Chicken (canned chunk)
Chili
Clams
Condensed Soups
Evaporated Milk
French Fried Onions
Gravy
Ham (canned chunk)
Instant Bouillon Granules
Miscellaneous Vegetables
Olive & Vegetable Oil
Salmon
Shrimp
Soy Sauce
Spaghetti Sauce
Tomatoes (juice, paste, sauce, stewed, whole)
Tuna
Vinegar
Worcestershire Sauce

Dry Products

All-purpose Flour
Bread Crumbs
Cornflake Crumbs
Cornstarch
Crackers
Croutons
Dried Herbs
Dried Potato Mixes
Dried Salad Dressing Mixes
Dried Soup Mixes
Flavored Noodle Mixes
Flavored Rice Mixes
Herb Seasoned Stuffing Mix
Instant Minced Onion
Instant Potato Flakes
Instant Rice
Nuts (chopped and sliced)
Pasta (Assorted Shapes and Assorted Noodles)
Salt & Pepper
Sauce Mixes
Seasoning Mixes (Beef Stew, Chow Mein, Taco)
Spices
Sugar
Rolled Oats

Refrigerator Storage Chart

Type	Storage Time Range
Bacon	1 week
Chicken in Broth or Gravy, cooked & leftover	1 to 2 days
Chopped Onion	3 to 5 days
Cream Cheese	2 weeks
Eggs	3 weeks
Green Chilies, canned	3 days
Ground Meats & Stew Meats, fresh	1 to 2 days
Ham Slices, fully cooked	3 days
Main Dishes, Beef, Pork, Lamb & Poultry, cooked & leftover	3 to 4 days
Main Dishes, Fish & Seafood, cooked & leftover	1 to 2 days
Meats (Beef, Pork, Lamb, Veal), fresh	3 to 5 days
Poultry, fresh	1 to 2 days
Tomato Paste	1 week

How to Stock the Refrigerator

Bacon	Garlic
Barbecue Sauce	Green Pepper
Butter or Margarine	Lemon Juice (bottled)
Carrots	Mayonnaise
Catsup	Milk
Celery	Mustard
Cheeses (cream cheese, assorted shredded packages, grated Parmesan cheese, processed spread or loaf)	Olives
	Onions
	Pickles
	Salad Dressings (French, Italian)
Chili Sauce	Salsa
Dairy Sour Cream	Steak Sauce
Eggs	Taco Sauce

Refrigerator Management

Compared to the pantry and freezer, your refrigerator is for short-term storage. It's the proper place for opened bottles of condiments, salad dressings or pickles. These items keep a long time, but not forever. The same is true for canned ham, cured meat and cheese. Most of the food in the refrigerator is renewed weekly. If you shop only once a week, it's important to store this food promptly and properly for maximum keeping quality. Choose dated products, like milk, eggs and meat, which will stay fresh until you are ready to use them. Place them in the refrigerator as soon as you bring them home. Keep fruits and vegetables in covered bins so they won't wilt or dry out. Some of them can be kept in plastic bags, but many need air or they will spoil. The covered bin or crisper allows them to 'breathe' while protecting them from the cold, dry air which circulates in the rest of the refrigerator.

Cover and refrigerate leftover cooked food as soon as the meal is over. Don't wait for hot foods to cool down or leave food out for latecomers. The microwave oven makes it easy to reheat single servings as they are needed. Until then, the safest place for leftovers is in the refrigerator.

Most leftovers can be stored in the refrigerator 3 to 4 days. The refrigerator storage chart offers guidelines on the length of time you can keep some fresh and cooked items. If the foods were not strictly fresh to start with, they will keep for a shorter time than indicated in the chart.

About Reheating

Many of the recipes in this book provide directions for reheating single servings.

Reheat foods in room temperature dishes. As food heats, it transfers heat to the container. If the dish is cold, the food will have to heat the dish before it will retain heat itself. This could result in overcooking and loss of fresh texture. Reheating times in this book are for refrigerated foods in room temperature containers.

Most foods can be reheated at High power. Solid pieces of meat, layered casseroles and foods containing cheese or cream are best heated at a lower power level, usually 70% (Medium High). Single servings usually do not require rotating. If your oven heats food unevenly, rotate the dish after half the reheating time.

How to Reheat Casseroles, Soups and Stews

Place one serving in room temperature plate or bowl. Spread main dish in shallow layer for fast, even heating.

Cover with wax paper or plastic wrap or another dish to hold in heat and moisture.

Microwave as directed in recipe, until the bottom of the dish feels very warm.

How to Reheat Combination Plates

Arrange foods on a room temperature plate with thick or dense foods to the outside of the dish.

Cover with wax paper or plastic wrap to hold in heat and retain moisture.

Microwave as directed in recipe, rotating the plate after half the time, if needed.

Fast and Easy From the Freezer

Efficient use of your freezer cuts down time-consuming trips to the supermarket. If you shop once a week, you can use the freezer for short-term storage of highly perishable foods like fish fillets, ground beef, pork or turkey which might not keep in the refrigerator until the day you plan to use them. Take advantage of supermarket specials by freezing your bargains for future use. Stock your freezer with frozen vegetables, vegetable combinations, chopped onion and peppers, breads and other items you use frequently in preparing main dishes or rounding out meals.

Precious after-work cooking time can be shortened by using foods which are partially prepared before they are frozen. Some of these main dishes can be completed from the frozen state. Others take a little time to defrost, but the time-consuming preparation is already done.

Making your own frozen entrees is another way to use your freezer for fast and easy meals. Entrees or leftovers may be frozen in convenient individual portions. Make a full recipe for four to six and freeze the extra portions for future meals.

Freezer Management

A full freezer costs less to operate than a nearly empty one. Once the food is frozen, it helps keep the freezer cold. There's less empty air to chill, so the freezer cycles on less often.

When you keep a full freezer, it's important that you know what you have there, keep track of its storage time and rotate the stock. Periodically, check the freezer contents and move older items to the top or front of the freezer, so you will use them within the recommended storage time.

Labeling is one of the essentials of good freezer management. Use a waterproof marker to date items you buy frozen, as well as those you freeze yourself. Choose either the date on which the item was purchased or frozen, or the date by which the food should be used for best quality, or indicate both dates. The chart suggests storage dates for foods kept in a freezer at 0°F.

The more information you provide on the label, the more time you'll save when defrosting and preparing the food. Include the type of food, the number of servings and the weight of meats which will be defrosted by minutes-per-pound.

Organizing the freezer is another way to save time in the long run. If you place food into the freezer hit or miss, you'll waste precious time hunting for it later. You may even forget that you have it.

Use wire baskets, open boxes, or even shopping bags to group similar items together in a chest freezer.

How to Stock the Freezer

Assorted Vegetables
Bulk Sausages
Chicken Breasts
Chicken Pieces
Cooked Cubed Meat
Cooked Rice
Fish Fillets
Ground Beef
Ground Turkey
Pork Chops
Seafood Sticks
Shrimp
Turkey Cutlets
Turkey Tenderloins
Frozen Fruit Bars
Ice Cream
Pre-baked Cakes
Pre-baked Cookies
Sherbet

Freezer Storage Chart

Type	Storage Time Range
Beef,	
Roasts	8 to 9 months
Ribs	3 to 4 months
Steaks	6 to 8 months
Ground	3 to 4 months
Pork,	
Roasts	4 to 6 months
Ribs	2 to 3 months
Chops	3 to 4 months
Ground	2 to 3 months
Ham,	
Fully Cooked	1 to 2 months
Sausage	1 to 2 months
Lamb,	
Chops	4 to 6 months
Ground	3 to 4 months
Poultry,	
Whole Chicken	6 to 8 months
Cut-up Chicken	6 to 8 months
Whole Boneless Turkey	6 to 8 months
Bone-in Turkey Breast	6 months
Turkey Tenderloins	3 months
Turkey Cutlets	3 months
Ground Turkey	3 months
Fish / Seafood,	
Fish Fillets (¾ to 1 lb. pkg.)	1 to 2 months
Shrimp	1 to 2 months
Seafood Sticks	1 month
Other Items,	
Breads	1 to 2 months
Cooked Rice	1 month
Cut-up Cooked Meat	2 to 3 months
Frozen Vegetables	6 months

Allocate shelf space to major food categories in an upright freezer. Labels on the shelves will remind you where to store poultry, meat or prepared foods, and assist others who may need to locate special items.

Freezer Packaging

If you want frozen foods to be as good when you use them as they were when you froze them, packaging is just as important as food quality. Time spent on proper packaging not only protects your food investment, it can speed defrosting later.

Packages must be airtight and the packaging material must be moisture and vapor proof. When you purchase already frozen items, like poultry or fish fillets, check the packages for tears. Air inside or outside of the package leaches moisture from the food, causing the hard, dry patches called freezer burn.

Freeze pre-packaged fresh poultry and meats in the original package if they will be stored frozen for a week or two. For extra protection, you may place the unopened package in a freezer-weight plastic bag or overwrap with heavy-duty foil or freezer paper. For longer storage, discard the original wrapping and re-package with heavy-duty foil or freezer paper.

There are several packaging techniques which will speed defrosting later, when time may be critical. Make packages no more than three inches thick for rapid, even defrosting. Where possible, use packaging to facilitate separation of pieces.

With partially prepared foods, indicate recipe name or page, or additional ingredients needed to complete the dish.

Packaging Cooked Foods

Whether they're made for the freezer or leftovers, cooked foods should be cooled before they are packaged and placed in the freezer. Airtight packaging is just as important for prepared foods as it is for uncooked foods. However, saucy or liquid items may expand during freezing.

Divide bulk packages of chicken pieces, pork chops or ground beef into recipe-size quantities. Stack chops, patties or pieces with a double thickness of wax paper or freezer paper between layers.

Another way to keep pieces separate is to spread them on a wax paper-lined tray and freeze individually before packaging.

Pack pre-frozen or layered items in freezer-weight plastic bags or wrap in heavy-duty foil or freezer paper. Press out as much air as possible before sealing and labeling.

How to Package Cooked Foods

Leave ½ inch of head space at the top of pint containers and 1 inch for quart containers. When sealing saucy items in bags, press out as much air as possible, then seal above the head space. Wrap solid individual items airtight in plastic wrap, then overwrap with heavy-duty foil or freezer paper.

Measure cubed cooked beef, pork or chicken into recipe-ready 2-cup portions. Place the cubes in a freezer bag or rigid plastic freezer container. If desired, add ¼ cup broth to protect meat from freezer burn. Seal and label.

About Defrosting

Whenever possible, packaging should be removed before defrosting. This makes it easier to break apart or separate foods and shortens defrosting time.

Overwraps of foil or freezer paper are easy to remove. Plastic underwraps can usually be peeled off. Occasionally, supermarket packaging or freezer bags may stick to the food. If this occurs, start defrosting and remove the packaging as soon as it loosens.

If the food is frozen in a plastic freezer container, place the container under hot running water until the block of food can be popped out. Open freezer bags or slit pouches and place them in a baking dish. If directions call for breaking up the food with a fork during defrosting, remove the bag as soon as food starts to soften.

How to Defrost Cubed or Ground Meat

Remove packaging. Place meat in 1-quart casserole. Defrost as directed in chart, pages 16-17.

Break apart as soon as possible. Remove any defrosted portions.

Defrost remaining time, breaking up again, if necessary. Let stand 5 minutes, until meat is cool but not icy.

How to Defrost Chops or Pieces

Remove packaging. Separate stacked items with table knife. Place meat on roasting rack.

Defrost for half the time, as directed in chart, pages 16-17. Separate pieces, if necessary. Turn pieces over and rearrange.

Defrost remaining time. Let stand for 10 to 15 minutes, or until meat is pliable and cool but not icy.

Defrosting Meat

Type	Power Level	Time	Procedure
Beef, Pork & Lamb			
Large Roasts, Flat Roasts & Large Steaks	50% (Med.)	5½ to 9 min./lb.	Unwrap and place on roasting rack. Microwave for ¼ of time. Shield if needed. Turn meat over. Microwave another ¼ of time. Let stand 10 minutes. Microwave remaining time, turning over once, until cool but not icy and skewer can be inserted into center. Let stand 20 to 30 minutes.
Ribs & Chops	50% (Med.)	3 to 6½ min./lb.	Unwrap and place on roasting rack. Microwave for half of time. Separate, turn over and rearrange. Microwave remaining time until cool but not icy. Let stand 10 to 15 minutes.
Ground	50% (Med.)	4 to 6 min./lb.	Unwrap and place in 1-quart casserole. Microwave, removing defrosted portions to another dish. Let stand 5 minutes.
Cooked Cubed Meat (2 cups) (Beef, Pork, Fully Cooked Ham or Turkey)	50% (Med.)	4 to 6 min.	Unwrap and place in 1-quart casserole. Microwave for half of time. Remove defrosted portions to another dish. Microwave remaining time until cool but not icy. Let stand 5 minutes.

Defrosting Fish & Shellfish

Type	Power Level	Time	Procedure
Fish			
Fillets, block	50% (Med.)	6 to 10 min./lb.	Unwrap and place in baking dish or on roasting rack. Microwave for half of time. Separate fillets as soon as possible. Microwave remaining time until fish is pliable but still icy. Let stand 10 minutes.
Fillets, individual	50% (Med.)	5 to 8 min./lb.	Unwrap and arrange on roasting rack. Microwave for half of time. Rearrange once. Microwave remaining time until fish is pliable but still icy. Let stand 10 minutes.
Steaks	50% (Med.)	4 to 7 min./lb.	Unwrap and place in baking dish or on roasting rack. Microwave for half of time. Separate and rearrange. Shield thin portions. Microwave remaining time until fish is pliable but icy in center. Let stand 5 to 10 minutes.
Scallops	50% (Med.)	4½ to 6 min./lb.	Unwrap and place in baking dish. Microwave for half of time. Separate scallops as soon as possible. Microwave remaining time until cold but not icy, stirring 2 or 3 times. Rinse with cold water. Let stand 5 minutes.
Shrimp Shelled, deveined	50% (Med.)	4 to 8 min./lb.	Unwrap and place in baking dish. Microwave for half of time. Separate shrimp as soon as possible. Microwave remaining time until cold but not icy, stirring 2 or 3 times. Rinse with cold water. Let stand 5 minutes.

Defrosting Poultry

Type	Power Level	Time	Procedure
Chicken			
Whole	30% (Med. Low)	5 to 9 min./lb.	Unwrap and place breast-side down in baking dish. Cover with wax paper. Microwave for half of time. Turn breast-side up. Shield if needed. Microwave remaining time. Remove giblets. Let stand 5 to 10 minutes until cool but not icy.
Quarters, Legs, Thighs, Wings	50% (Med.)	4 to 6½ min./lb.	Unwrap and place in baking dish or on roasting rack. Microwave for half of time. Separate pieces. Arrange with thickest portions toward outside. Microwave remaining time. Let stand 10 to 15 minutes until cool but not icy.
Boneless Breasts	50% (Med.)	5½ to 8 min./lb.	Unwrap and place in baking dish or on roasting rack. Microwave for half of time. Separate pieces. Microwave remaining time until pliable but cold. Let stand 15 to 20 minutes.
Turkey			
Whole, boneless, 4 lbs.	50% (Med.)	7½ to 9½ min./lb.	Unwrap and place on roasting rack. Microwave for half of time, turning over once. Let stand 15 minutes. Remove gravy packet. Turn turkey over. Microwave remaining time, turning over once. Let stand 20 minutes until cool but not icy.
Bone-in Breast	50% (Med.)	3½ to 5½ min./lb.	Unwrap and place skin-side down on roasting rack. Microwave for half of time. Remove gravy packet. Turn skin-side up. Shield if needed. Microwave remaining time. Rinse in cool water. Let stand 5 to 10 minutes until cool but not icy.
Tenderloins	50% (Med.)	4 to 6 min./lb.	Unwrap and place on roasting rack. Microwave for half of time. Shield thin portions. Microwave remaining time. Let stand 10 to 15 minutes until cool but not icy.
Cutlets	30% (Med. Low)	7 to 11 min./lb.	Unwrap and place on roasting rack. Microwave for half of time. Separate and rearrange as soon as possible. Microwave remaining time, until pliable but still icy. Let stand to complete defrosting.
Ground	50% (Med.)	4 to 6 min./lb.	Unwrap and place in casserole. Microwave, removing defrosted portions to another dish. Let stand 10 minutes.
Cornish Hens	50% (Med.)	5 to 7 min./lb.	Unwrap and place breast-side down in baking dish. Cover with wax paper. Microwave for half of time. Turn breast-side up. Shield if needed. Rearrange hens. Microwave remaining time. Remove giblets. Let stand 5 minutes.

Family Favorites

Lemony Fillets & Rice

Beef

◄ **Tangy Round Steak**

- 1½- lb. boneless beef top round steak, about 1 inch thick
- 1 tablespoon all-purpose flour
- 1 medium onion, thinly sliced
- 1 clove garlic, minced
- ½ cup French dressing
- 1 tablespoon lemon juice
- 1 teaspoon Worcestershire sauce
- ½ teaspoon bouquet sauce (optional)
- ¼ teaspoon dried thyme leaves
- ⅛ teaspoon pepper

4 to 6 servings

Pierce steak thoroughly with fork. Place flour in nylon cooking bag. Shake to coat. Add steak. Top with onion and garlic. Set aside. In 1-cup measure, combine remaining ingredients. Pour mixture over steak. Secure bag with nylon tie or string. Place bag on plate. Refrigerate for at least 8 hours or overnight.

Place steak in bag in 9-inch square baking dish. Microwave at High for 5 minutes. Microwave at 50% (Medium) for 30 to 40 minutes, or until beef is tender, turning steak over once. Let stand, covered, for 10 minutes. Cut into thin slices and serve with sauce.

To reheat: Place one serving on plate. Cover with wax paper. Microwave at 70% (Medium High) for 1½ to 2½ minutes, or until heated through.

Tangy Round Steak
Mashed Potatoes
Green Beans & Water Chestnuts
Angel Food Cake with Strawberries

Family Swiss Steak ▲

- 1½- lb. boneless beef top round steak, about ¾ inch thick, trimmed and cut into serving-size pieces
- 3 tablespoons all-purpose flour
- 1 teaspoon dried parsley flakes
- ¼ teaspoon dried thyme leaves
- ⅛ teaspoon pepper
- 1 can (10½ oz.) condensed French onion soup
- 1 medium onion, thinly sliced
- 1 medium carrot, cut into 1½ × ¼-inch strips

4 servings

Pound each piece of beef to ¼-inch thickness. Set aside. In large plastic food storage bag, combine flour, parsley, thyme and pepper. Add beef. Shake to coat. Arrange pieces in 10-inch square casserole. Pour soup over beef. Top with onion and carrot. Cover. Microwave at High for 5 minutes. Microwave at 50% (Medium) for 35 to 40 minutes, or until beef is tender, turning pieces over and stirring sauce once. Let stand, covered, for 10 minutes.

To reheat: Place one serving on plate. Cover with wax paper. Microwave at 70% (Medium High) for 3½ to 4 minutes, or until heated through.

Family Swiss Steak
Rice Medley   Broiled Tomatoes   Coleslaw   Peach Crisp

Creamy Cubed Steak Casserole

- 1 pkg. (10 oz.) frozen Brussels sprouts
- 4 beef cubed steaks (4 to 5 oz. each)
- 2⅓ cups hot water
- ⅔ cup milk
- 1 tablespoon butter or margarine
- 1 pkg. (5.75 oz.) creamy Italian potatoes mix

4 servings

Unwrap Brussels sprouts and place on plate. Microwave at High for 3 to 4 minutes, or until defrosted. Drain. Set aside. Place beef in 10-inch square casserole. Cover. Microwave at High for 3 minutes. Turn beef over. Microwave at High for 3 to 5 minutes, or until outside of beef is no longer pink. Drain. Set aside.

Place water in 4-cup measure. Microwave at High for 4 to 7 minutes, or until water boils. Stir in milk, butter, potatoes and sauce packet. Mix well. Pour mixture evenly over beef cubed steaks. Cover. Microwave at High for 5 minutes. Stir. Microwave at 70% (Medium High) for 10 minutes. Stir in Brussels sprouts. Re-cover. Microwave at 70% (Medium High) for 10 to 13 minutes, or until beef is tender and sauce thickens.

To reheat: Place one serving on plate. Cover with wax paper. Microwave at 70% (Medium High) for 2½ to 3½ minutes, or until heated through.

Salsa-marinated Ribs ▲

- 1 tablespoon all-purpose flour
- 3½ to 4 lbs. beef short ribs, trimmed
- 1 cup hot salsa
- 1 stalk celery, cut into 1-inch pieces
- ½ teaspoon chili powder

4 servings

Place flour in nylon cooking bag. Shake to coat. Add ribs, salsa and celery. Sprinkle with chili powder. Secure bag with nylon tie or string. Place bag on plate. Refrigerate for at least 8 hours or overnight, turning bag over twice.

Place ribs in bag in 10-inch square casserole. Microwave at High for 5 minutes. Microwave at 70% (Medium High) for 40 to 55 minutes, or until beef is tender, turning ribs over and rearranging twice. Let stand, covered, for 10 minutes.

To reheat: Place one serving on plate. Cover with wax paper. Microwave at 70% (Medium High) for 2½ to 4 minutes, or until heated through.

Salsa-marinated Ribs
Scalloped Potatoes   Spinach & Orange Salad   Chocolate Pudding

Creamy Cubed Steak Casserole
Sliced Marinated Tomatoes & Onions
Gingerbread with Whipped Topping

Fast & Easy Beef Stew

- 1 lb. beef cubed steaks, cut into 1-inch pieces
- 1 tablespoon vegetable oil
- 1 clove garlic, minced
- 1 envelope (1.5 oz.) beef stew seasoning mix
- ¼ cup all-purpose flour
- 1 teaspoon salt
- 2 cups water
- 1 pkg. (1½ lbs.) frozen stew vegetables
- 1 tablespoon dried parsley flakes

4 to 6 servings

In 2-quart casserole, combine beef pieces, oil and garlic. Cover. Microwave at High for 5 to 7 minutes, or until beef is no longer pink, stirring once. Stir in stew seasoning mix, flour and salt. Stir in water, vegetables and parsley. Re-cover. Microwave at High for 5 minutes. Stir. Re-cover. Microwave at 70% (Medium High) for 25 to 30 minutes, or until mixture thickens and beef and vegetables are tender, stirring twice. Let stand, covered, for 5 to 10 minutes.

To reheat: Place one serving in bowl. Cover with wax paper. Microwave at High for 4½ to 6 minutes, or until heated through, stirring once.

Fast & Easy Beef Stew
Corn Bread with Butter & Honey   Cherry Pie

Beef Strips & Sour Cream Gravy

- ¾ cup water
- 1 can (4 oz.) sliced mushrooms, drained
- 1 envelope (.87 oz.) onion gravy mix
- ½ cup shredded carrot
- 1 tablespoon dried parsley flakes
- 1 tablespoon catsup
- 1 teaspoon Worcestershire sauce
- 1½- lb. boneless beef sirloin steak, about 1 inch thick, cut into thin strips*
- 1 cup dairy sour cream

4 to 6 servings

In 1½-quart casserole, combine water, mushrooms, gravy mix, carrot, parsley, catsup and Worcestershire sauce. Cover. Microwave at High for 6 to 8 minutes, or until mixture thickens, stirring twice. Stir in beef strips. Re-cover. Microwave at 70% (Medium High) for 7 to 11 minutes, or until beef is tender and no longer pink, stirring twice. Blend in sour cream. Let stand, covered, for 5 minutes.

*Freeze beef partially for easier slicing.

To reheat: Place one serving in bowl. Cover with wax paper. Microwave at 50% (Medium) for 3½ to 5 minutes, or until heated through, stirring once.

Beef Strips & Sour Cream Gravy
Egg Noodles   Green Beans   Cloverleaf Rolls   Cherry Pie

Deli Beef Rolls ▶

- ½ cup chopped onion
- ⅓ cup chopped celery
- ¼ cup plus 2 tablespoons finely shredded carrot, divided
- 3 tablespoons butter or margarine
- 1¼ cups herb seasoned stuffing mix
- ¼ cup chopped walnuts (optional)
- ¼ cup hot water
- 4 large slices cooked beef roast (about 1 lb.) ¼ to ½ inch thick
- ¾ cup beef gravy
- ½ teaspoon Worcestershire sauce

4 servings

In 1-quart casserole, combine onion, celery, ¼ cup carrot and the butter. Cover. Microwave at High for 3 to 4½ minutes, or until vegetables are tender-crisp. Stir in stuffing mix and walnuts. Mix in water. Place about one-fourth of stuffing on each slice of beef. Roll up, enclosing stuffing. Place beef rolls seam-side down in 9×5-inch loaf dish.

Place gravy in 1-cup measure. Stir in remaining 2 tablespoons carrot and the Worcestershire sauce. Pour gravy over beef rolls. Cover with wax paper. Microwave at 70% (Medium High) for 12 to 18 minutes, or until center of each beef roll is hot, rotating dish once.

Deli Beef Rolls
Rotini Pasta Salad
Carrot & Celery Sticks
Lemon Bars

Family Pleasin' Meatloaf

- 1½ lbs. ground beef
- ¾ cup rolled oats
- ½ cup milk
- 1 egg, slightly beaten
- 1 tablespoon instant minced onion
- 1 teaspoon salt
- ¼ teaspoon pepper
- ¼ teaspoon paprika
- 1 tablespoon chili sauce

6 servings

In medium mixing bowl, combine all ingredients, except chili sauce. Mix well. Shape into 8×4-inch loaf. Place loaf on roasting rack. Cover with wax paper. Microwave at High for 14 to 18 minutes, or until loaf is firm and internal temperature in center registers 150°F, rotating rack once or twice. Spread chili sauce over top of loaf. Microwave, uncovered, at 50% (Medium) for 1 minute. Cover with wax paper. Let stand for 10 minutes.

To reheat: Place one serving on plate. Cover with wax paper. Microwave at High for 2½ to 3 minutes, or until heated through.

Family Pleasin' Meatloaf
Baked Potatoes with Bacon Bits, Chives & Sour Cream
French-style Green Beans with Sliced Almonds
Apple Crisp

Cheesy Broccoli-stuffed Meatloaf

- 1½ lbs. lean ground beef
- 1 egg, slightly beaten
- ¼ cup plus 2 tablespoons seasoned dry bread crumbs, divided
- ¼ cup finely chopped onion, divided
- ¾ teaspoon salt, divided
- ½ teaspoon dried basil leaves
- ⅛ teaspoon pepper
- 1 cup frozen broccoli cuts
- ½ cup shredded cheese (Monterey Jack, Cheddar or mozzarella)
- 1 tablespoon butter or margarine
- ¼ teaspoon bouquet sauce

6 servings

Cheesy Broccoli-stuffed Meatloaf
Buttered New Potatoes
Lettuce Wedge with Italian Dressing
Sherbet & Assorted Cookies

How to Microwave Cheesy Broccoli-stuffed Meatloaf

Combine beef, egg, ¼ cup bread crumbs, 2 tablespoons onion, ½ teaspoon salt, the basil and pepper in medium mixing bowl. Mix well. Set aside. In 1-quart casserole, combine broccoli and remaining 2 tablespoons onion. Cover.

Microwave at High for 2 to 3 minutes, or until hot. Cool slightly. Cut broccoli into bite-size pieces. Stir in remaining 2 tablespoons bread crumbs, remaining ¼ teaspoon salt and the cheese. Set aside.

Place butter in custard cup. Microwave at High for 45 seconds to 1 minute, or until butter melts. Stir in bouquet sauce. Set aside.

Family Favorites/Beef

Press half of beef mixture into 8 × 4-inch loaf dish, forming an indentation in center and about 1-inch thickness on sides. Spoon broccoli mixture into center indentation.

Top with remaining beef mixture, pressing evenly and sealing edges. Brush butter mixture lightly over top of loaf. Cover with wax paper. Place dish on saucer in microwave oven. Microwave at High for 5 minutes. Rotate dish half turn. Brush with remaining butter mixture. Re-cover.

Microwave at 70% (Medium High) for 11 to 15 minutes, or until bottom center of loaf appears cooked and internal temperature in center of loaf registers 150°F, rotating dish once or twice. Let stand, covered, for 5 minutes.

Salisbury Steak with Mushroom Sauce

- 1 lb. ground beef
- 1 cup soft bread crumbs
- 1 egg, slightly beaten
- 3 tablespoons milk
- 1 teaspoon dried parsley flakes
- ½ teaspoon salt
- ⅛ teaspoon garlic powder
- ⅛ teaspoon pepper

Mushroom Sauce:
- 1¼ cups milk
- 1 envelope (⅞ oz.) mushroom sauce mix
- 1 teaspoon dried parsley flakes

4 servings

In medium mixing bowl, combine beef, bread crumbs, egg, 3 tablespoons milk, the parsley, salt, garlic powder and pepper. Mix well. Shape into 4 oval patties, about 4½ × 2½ inches each. Arrange patties in 9-inch square baking dish. Cover with wax paper. Microwave at High for 7 to 10 minutes, or until patties are firm and no longer pink in center, rotating dish once. Drain. Set aside.

Place milk in 2-cup measure. Stir in sauce mix and parsley. Microwave at High for 4 to 6 minutes, or until sauce thickens, stirring 2 or 3 times. Pour sauce over patties. Cover with wax paper. Microwave at 50% (Medium) for 2 to 3 minutes, or until heated through.

To reheat: Place one serving on plate. Cover with wax paper. Microwave at 70% (Medium High) for 3½ to 5 minutes, or until heated through.

Salisbury Steak with Mushroom Sauce

Thin Egg Noodles
Zucchini & Summer Squash
Pound Cake with Rhubarb Sauce

Meat & Potato Bake ▲

- 1 lb. ground beef
- ½ cup herb seasoned stuffing mix
- 1 egg, slightly beaten
- ¼ cup sliced green onions, divided
- ¼ teaspoon pepper
- Dash ground allspice
- ¾ cup milk
- 1 can (10¾ oz.) condensed creamy potato soup

4 servings

In medium mixing bowl, combine beef, stuffing mix, egg, 2 tablespoons onions, the pepper and allspice. Mix well. Shape into 4 loaves, about 3½ × 2 inches each. Arrange loaves in 9-inch square baking dish. Cover with wax paper. Microwave at High for 7 to 11 minutes, or until loaves are firm and no longer pink in center, rotating dish once. Drain. Set aside. In 4-cup measure, combine milk, soup and remaining 2 tablespoons onions. Spoon mixture over loaves. Cover with wax paper. Microwave at 50% (Medium) for 7 to 11 minutes, or until sauce is heated, spooning sauce over loaves once.

Meat & Potato Bake

Broccoli, Cauliflower, Carrot & Pea Pod Medley
Brownies

Italian Meatball Dinner ▶

1 lb. ground beef
1 egg, slightly beaten
3 tablespoons seasoned dry bread crumbs
2 teaspoons instant minced onion
¼ teaspoon salt
1 pkg. (4.5 oz.) shell pasta with herb and tomato sauce mix
2 cups hot water
1 can (4 oz.) sliced mushrooms, drained
1 cup shredded mozzarella cheese
1 teaspoon dried parsley flakes

4 servings

In medium mixing bowl, combine beef, egg, bread crumbs, onion and salt. Mix well. Shape into 12 meatballs, about 1½ inches each. Place meatballs in 2-quart casserole. Cover. Microwave at High for 6 to 7 minutes, or until meatballs are firm and no longer pink. Drain.

Stir in remaining ingredients, except cheese and parsley. Re-cover. Microwave at High for 13 to 15 minutes, or until pasta is tender and sauce thickens, stirring once. Sprinkle with cheese and parsley. Re-cover. Microwave at 50% (Medium) for 1 to 2 minutes, or until cheese melts. Let stand, covered, for 3 minutes.

To reheat: Place one serving on plate. Cover with wax paper. Microwave at High for 2 to 3 minutes, or until heated through.

Italian Meatball Dinner
Buttered Broccoli Spears with Pimiento
Garlic Bread
Rainbow Sherbet

Chinese Chow Mein

½ lb. ground beef
½ cup chopped onion
½ cup water
1 envelope (1⅛ oz.) chow mein seasoning mix
1 can (16 oz.) chow mein vegetables, drained
1 can (4 oz.) mushroom pieces and stems, drained

2 to 4 servings

Crumble beef into 1½-quart casserole. Add onion. Cover. Microwave at High for 3 to 4½ minutes, or until beef is no longer pink, stirring once to break apart. Stir in water and seasoning mix. Microwave, uncovered, at High for 4 to 10 minutes, or until mixture thickens and bubbles, stirring once. Stir in chow mein vegetables and mushrooms. Cover. Microwave at High for 3 to 5 minutes, or until heated through, stirring once. Serve over crisp noodles.

To reheat: Place one serving in bowl. Cover with wax paper. Microwave at High for 2 to 3 minutes, or until heated through, stirring once.

Chinese Chow Mein
White Rice   Lettuce & Mandarin Orange Salad
Almond or Fortune Cookies

Mediterranean Layered Casserole

- 1 lb. ground beef, or ½ lb. ground lamb plus ½ lb. ground beef
- 2 teaspoons instant minced onion
- ⅓ cup tomato sauce
- ½ teaspoon ground cinnamon
- ½ teaspoon salt, divided
- ¼ teaspoon pepper, divided
- 1 pkg. (4.75 oz.) cream-style potatoes mix
- 1⅓ cups milk
- 1 cup water
- 1 cup ricotta cheese
- ¼ cup grated Parmesan cheese
- 1 egg, slightly beaten
- 2 teaspoons dried parsley flakes

6 servings

Mediterranean Layered Casserole

*Spinach with Lemon Butter
Marinated Vegetable Salad
Sugar Cookies*

How to Microwave Mediterranean Layered Casserole

Crumble beef into 1-quart casserole. Add onion. Cover. Microwave at High for 4 to 7 minutes, or until beef is no longer pink, stirring once to break apart. Drain.

Stir in tomato sauce, cinnamon, ¼ teaspoon salt and ⅛ teaspoon pepper. Set aside.

Combine potatoes and sauce packet, milk and water in 9-inch square baking dish. Cover with plastic wrap. Microwave at High for 5 minutes. Stir. Microwave, uncovered, at High for 8 to 13 minutes, or until potatoes are tender and sauce thickens, stirring once.

Layer beef mixture over potatoes. Set aside. In small mixing bowl, combine ricotta and Parmesan cheeses, egg, remaining ¼ teaspoon salt, remaining ⅛ teaspoon pepper and the parsley. Mix well.

Spread cheese mixture evenly over beef layer. Cover with wax paper.

Microwave at High for 6 to 9 minutes, or until center is hot and cheese mixture appears set, rotating dish once. Let stand, covered, for 5 to 10 minutes.

Family Favorites/Beef

Cheesy Mac & Burger

- 1½ cups uncooked elbow macaroni
- ⅓ cup chopped onion
- ¼ cup chopped green pepper
- ½ lb. ground beef
- 1 pkg. (8 oz.) pasteurized process cheese spread, cut into ¾-inch cubes
- 1 can (16 oz.) whole tomatoes, drained and cut up
- ¼ cup milk
- ½ teaspoon salt
- ¼ teaspoon dried marjoram leaves (optional)
- ⅛ teaspoon pepper
- Paprika (optional)

4 to 6 servings

Prepare macaroni as directed on package. Rinse and drain. Set aside. In 2-quart casserole, combine onion and green pepper. Cover. Microwave at High for 3 minutes. Crumble beef over vegetables. Re-cover. Microwave at High for 2 to 4 minutes, or until beef is no longer pink, stirring once to break apart.

Stir in macaroni and remaining ingredients, except paprika. Re-cover. Microwave at High for 6 to 8 minutes, or until heated through and cheese melts, stirring twice. Sprinkle with paprika.

To reheat: Place one serving on plate. Cover with wax paper. Microwave at High for 1½ to 3 minutes, or until heated through, stirring once.

Cheesy Mac & Burger
Three-Bean Salad
Bran Muffins
Apple Wedges

Beef-n-Beans

- ¼ cup chopped onion
- ¼ cup finely chopped celery
- 1 clove garlic, minced
- 1 lb. ground beef
- 1 can (16 oz.) pork and beans
- ¼ cup chili sauce
- ¼ cup tomato juice
- 2 tablespoons finely chopped dill pickle
- ½ teaspoon salt
- ½ teaspoon Worcestershire sauce
- ⅛ teaspoon pepper

4 to 6 servings

In 1½-quart casserole, combine onion, celery and garlic. Cover. Microwave at High for 3 minutes. Crumble beef over vegetables. Re-cover. Microwave at High for 4 to 6 minutes, or until beef is no longer pink, stirring once to break apart. Drain. Stir in remaining ingredients. Mix well. Re-cover. Microwave at High for 3 to 6 minutes, or until hot and flavors are blended, stirring once.

To reheat: Place one serving in bowl. Cover with wax paper. Microwave at High for 2 to 3 minutes, or until heated through, stirring once.

Beef-n-Beans
Coleslaw   Texas Toast   Strawberry Ice Cream

Southwestern Chili Pie

Crust:
- 1 can (15 oz.) Spanish rice, well-drained
- ½ cup unseasoned dry bread crumbs
- 1 egg, slightly beaten

Filling:
- ½ lb. ground beef
- 1 can (15 oz.) chili with beans
- 1 can (4 oz.) chopped green chilies, drained
- ¾ cup finely crushed corn chips
- 2 tablespoons sliced black olives
- ½ cup shredded Cheddar cheese

6 servings

Southwestern Chili Pie
Lettuce, Tomato & Black Olive Salad with Ranch Dressing
Tortilla Chips
Lemon Sherbet

How to Microwave Southwestern Chili Pie

Combine all crust ingredients in small mixing bowl. Mix well. Spread evenly against bottom and sides of 9-inch pie plate. Microwave at High for 4 to 7 minutes, or until crust appears dry and set, rotating plate once. Set aside.

Crumble beef into 1-quart casserole. Microwave at High for 2 to 4 minutes, or until beef is no longer pink, stirring once to break apart. Drain. Stir in chili, green chilies, corn chips, and olives. Spread mixture evenly into crust.

Cover with wax paper. Microwave at High for 7 to 11 minutes, or until center is hot, rotating plate once. Sprinkle cheese over pie. Microwave, uncovered, at 50% (Medium) for 2½ to 4 minutes, or until cheese melts. Serve with dairy sour cream, guacamole and taco sauce, if desired.

Family Favorites/Beef 33

◀ **Burger & Creamy Noodles**

- 3 cups uncooked wide egg noodles
- 1 lb. ground beef
- 1 cup chopped celery
- ½ cup chopped onion
- ¼ cup chopped green pepper
- 1 can (10¾ oz.) condensed cream of mushroom soup
- 1 pkg. (3 oz.) cream cheese, cut into ½-inch cubes
- ¾ teaspoon garlic salt
- ⅛ teaspoon pepper
- 1 can (8 oz.) whole kernel corn, drained
- 1 can (2.8 oz.) French fried onions

4 to 6 servings

Prepare noodles as directed on package. Rinse and drain. Set aside. Crumble beef into 2-quart casserole. Stir in celery, onion and green pepper. Cover. Microwave at High for 4 to 7 minutes, or until beef is no longer pink, stirring once to break apart. Drain.

Stir in soup, cream cheese, garlic salt and pepper. Mix in noodles and corn. Re-cover. Microwave at High for 8 to 10 minutes, or until vegetables are tender, stirring once. Sprinkle with onions. Microwave, uncovered, at High for 2 minutes, or until heated through.

To reheat: Place one serving on plate. Cover with wax paper. Microwave at High for 2 to 3 minutes, or until heated through, stirring once.

> *Burger & Creamy Noodles*
> Marinated Vegetables
> Garlic Toast
> Individual Strawberry Shortcakes

Speedy Burger & Rice

- 1 lb. ground beef
- ½ cup chopped onion
- 1 pkg. (8 oz.) beef-flavored rice and vermicelli mix (reserve seasoning packet)
- 2 tablespoons butter or margarine
- 3 cups hot water
- ¼ teaspoon salt
- ¼ teaspoon pepper
- 1 cup frozen peas
- 2 tablespoons sliced pimiento (optional)

4 to 6 servings

Crumble beef into 2-quart casserole. Add onion. Cover. Microwave at High for 4 to 7 minutes, or until beef is no longer pink, stirring once to break apart. Drain. Set aside. In same casserole, combine rice and vermicelli and butter. Microwave, uncovered, at High for 4 to 6 minutes, or until vermicelli is light brown, stirring 2 or 3 times. Stir in water, seasoning packet, salt and pepper. Cover. Microwave at High for 5 to 10 minutes, or until mixture thickens and liquid is partially absorbed. Mix in beef, peas and pimiento. Re-cover. Microwave at High for 5 to 7 minutes, or until rice and peas are tender.

To reheat: Place one serving on plate. Cover with wax paper. Microwave at High for 1½ to 3 minutes, or until heated through, stirring once.

> *Speedy Burger & Rice*
> Tomato & Cucumber Salad   Parker House Rolls
> Gingersnaps

Reuben Bake

- 2 cups hot water
- 1 pkg. (4.5 oz.) butter-flavored noodles and sauce mix
- 1 teaspoon instant minced onion
- 1 can (12 oz.) corned beef, chopped, or 1½ cups chopped sliced corned beef
- 1 can (16 oz.) sauerkraut, rinsed and drained
- ¼ cup thousand island dressing
- 1 cup shredded Swiss cheese
- 1 teaspoon dried parsley flakes
- 1 cup unseasoned whole wheat and white croutons

4 to 6 servings

Reuben Bake
Zucchini & Summer Squash Sticks
Rye or Whole Wheat Dinner Rolls
Baked Apples

How to Microwave Reuben Bake

Place water in 2-quart casserole. Cover. Microwave at High for 4 to 7 minutes, or until water boils. Stir in noodles and sauce mix and onion. Microwave, uncovered, at High for 7 to 9 minutes, or until sauce thickens, stirring twice.

Layer corned beef, sauerkraut and dressing over noodles and sauce. Cover. Microwave at 70% (Medium High) for 7 to 9 minutes, or until center is hot, rotating casserole once.

Sprinkle cheese, parsley and croutons over noodles. Microwave, uncovered, at 70% (Medium High) for 3 to 4 minutes, or until cheese melts, rotating casserole once. Let stand for 5 minutes.

Creamy Rice & Beef Dinner

- 1 pkg. (4.6 oz.) beef-flavored rice and sauce mix
- 1 can (10¾ oz.) condensed creamy cauliflower soup
- 1¾ cups hot water
- 2 tablespoons finely chopped onion
- 2 cups cubed cooked beef, ½-inch cubes
- 1 cup frozen peas and carrots

4 to 6 servings

In 1½-quart casserole, combine rice and sauce mix, soup, water and onion. Mix well. Cover. Microwave at High for 15 to 19 minutes, or just until rice is tender, stirring 2 or 3 times. Stir in beef and peas and carrots. Re-cover. Microwave at High for 5 to 6 minutes, or until peas and carrots are hot. Let stand, covered, for 5 minutes.

Creamy Rice & Beef Dinner
Tossed Lettuce & Spinach Salad with Radish Slices & French Dressing
Raspberry Gelatin with Raspberries

How to Microwave Smoked Beef-stuffed Peppers

◀ Smoked Beef-stuffed Peppers

- 4 medium green peppers
- 1 pkg. (4.4 oz.) broccoli, au gratin rice mix
- ½ cup chopped carrot
- 2 tablespoons butter or margarine
- ¼ teaspoon Italian seasoning
- 1¾ cups hot water
- 1 pkg. (2.5 oz.) smoked sliced beef, cut into ½-inch strips
- 2 tablespoons chopped pecans

4 servings

Smoked Beef-stuffed Peppers
Marinated Cucumber Salad
Crescent Rolls
Chocolate Cake with White Frosting

Slice tops from green peppers and remove seeds. Remove thin slice from bottom of each pepper to allow peppers to stand upright. Place cut-side up in 9-inch square baking dish. Set aside.

Combine rice and seasoning packet, carrot, butter, Italian seasoning and water in 2-quart casserole. Cover. Microwave at High for 5 minutes. Stir. Re-cover.

Microwave at 50% (Medium) for 20 to 30 minutes, or until liquid is absorbed and rice is tender. Stir in beef.

Fill each pepper with about ¾ cup rice mixture. Cover with plastic wrap. Microwave at High for 8 to 10 minutes, or until peppers are tender, rotating dish once.

Sprinkle pecans over stuffing. Let stand, covered, for 2 to 3 minutes before serving.

Pork

Quick Creole Chops

- 4 pork chops (4 to 5 oz. each) ½ inch thick
- 2 tablespoons all-purpose flour
- 1 cup sliced zucchini, ¼ inch thick
- ½ cup red or green pepper pieces, 1-inch pieces
- 1 can (16 oz.) stewed tomatoes
- ¼ cup chili sauce
- 1 teaspoon sugar
- ¼ teaspoon dried thyme leaves
- ⅛ teaspoon cayenne

4 servings

Place chops in large plastic food storage bag. Add flour. Shake to coat. Arrange chops in 9-inch square baking dish with bone-side toward center of dish. Add any excess flour to dish. Top with zucchini and red pepper. Set aside.

In small mixing bowl, blend remaining ingredients. Pour over chops and vegetables. Cover with wax paper. Microwave at 70% (Medium High) for 20 to 28 minutes, or until pork near bone is no longer pink and sauce thickens, rotating dish once or twice. Let stand, covered, for 5 minutes.

To reheat: Place one serving on plate. Cover with wax paper. Microwave at 70% (Medium High) for 3½ to 4½ minutes, or until heated through.

Quick Creole Chops
Brown Rice
Melon & Banana Salad
Corn Bread with Butter & Honey
Custard with Caramel Sauce

Chops & Creamed Cabbage

- 4 pork chops (4 to 5 oz. each) ½ inch thick
- 4 cups sliced cabbage, ½ inch thick

Sauce:
- 3 tablespoons butter or margarine
- ¼ cup all-purpose flour
- ½ teaspoon salt
- ½ teaspoon dried marjoram leaves
- ¼ teaspoon pepper
- 1½ cups milk
- ¼ cup grated Parmesan cheese

4 servings

Brown chops conventionally on both sides. Place cabbage in 9-inch square baking dish. Arrange chops over cabbage with bone-side toward center of dish. Set aside.

Place butter in 4-cup measure. Microwave at High for 1 to 1¼ minutes, or until butter melts. Stir in flour, salt, marjoram and pepper. Blend in milk. Microwave at High for 4 to 5 minutes, or until mixture thickens and bubbles, stirring twice. Stir in Parmesan cheese.

Pour sauce over chops and cabbage. Cover with wax paper. Microwave at 70% (Medium High) for 14 to 18 minutes, or until pork near bone is no longer pink, rotating dish once or twice.

To reheat: Place one serving on plate. Cover with wax paper. Microwave at 70% (Medium High) for 3½ to 4½ minutes, or until heated through.

Barbecued Pork Slices ▲

- 1 cup diagonally sliced celery, ½ inch thick
- 1 small onion, cut into 8 pieces
- 1 can (8 oz.) tomato sauce
- ¼ cup steak sauce
- 2 tablespoons packed brown sugar
- ½ teaspoon dry mustard
- ½ teaspoon paprika
- ¼ teaspoon salt
- 6 slices cooked pork loin roast (about ¾ lb.) ¼ inch thick

2 to 4 servings

In 9-inch square baking dish, combine celery and onion. Cover with plastic wrap. Microwave at High for 5 to 6 minutes, or until vegetables are tender-crisp, stirring once. Stir in tomato sauce, steak sauce, brown sugar, dry mustard, paprika and salt. Mix well. Add sliced pork. Spoon sauce over pork. Cover with wax paper. Microwave at 50% (Medium) for 15 to 20 minutes, or until flavors are blended, spooning sauce over pork once or twice.

Barbecued Pork Slices
Potato Salad   Dilled Peas & Carrots   Hard Rolls
Spice Cake with Cream Cheese Frosting

Chops & Creamed Cabbage
Glazed Carrots
Whole Wheat Muffins
Cherry Pie

Teriyaki Orange Ribs

1 tablespoon all-purpose flour
4 lbs. pork spareribs, trimmed and cut into serving-size pieces
½ cup teriyaki sauce
2 tablespoons frozen orange juice concentrate
1 clove garlic, minced
¼ teaspoon ground ginger
⅛ teaspoon cayenne

4 servings

Place flour in nylon cooking bag. Shake to coat. Add ribs. In 1-cup measure, blend teriyaki sauce, orange juice concentrate, garlic, ginger and cayenne. Pour over ribs. Secure bag with string or nylon tie. Place bag on plate. Refrigerate for at least 8 hours or overnight.

Place ribs in bag in 10-inch square casserole. Microwave at High for 5 minutes. Microwave at 70% (Medium High) for 25 to 35 minutes, or until pork is tender, turning ribs over and rearranging twice. Let stand, covered, for 10 minutes.

To reheat: Place one serving on plate. Cover with wax paper. Microwave at 70% (Medium High) for 2½ to 4 minutes, or until heated through.

Teriyaki Orange Ribs
Fried Rice
Buttered Asparagus with Sesame Seed
Angel Food Cake with Plum Sauce

Hawaiian Patties

- 2 cans (6¾ oz. each) chunk ham, flaked
- 1 cup soft bread crumbs
- 1 egg, slightly beaten
- 1 can (8 oz.) crushed pineapple in juice, drained (reserve 1 tablespoon juice)
- ¼ cup sliced green onions, divided
- ¼ teaspoon pepper
- 1 tablespoon packed brown sugar
- 1 tablespoon prepared mustard

4 servings

Place ham in medium mixing bowl. Add bread crumbs, egg, crushed pineapple, 2 tablespoons onions and the pepper. Mix well. Shape into 4 patties, about ¾ inch thick. Place patties on roasting rack. Cover with wax paper. Microwave at 70% (Medium High) for 10 to 16 minutes, or until patties are firm, rotating rack once.

In small bowl, blend reserved pineapple juice, brown sugar and mustard. Stir in remaining 2 tablespoons onions. Spoon sauce over patties. Microwave at 50% (Medium) for 2 to 3 minutes, or until sauce is hot.

To reheat: Place one serving on plate. Cover with wax paper. Microwave at 70% (Medium High) for 2 to 3 minutes, or until heated through.

Hawaiian Patties
Oriental Vegetable Medley
Egg Rolls
Vanilla Ice Cream & Sugar Cookies

Fruited Ham Slice ▲

- 1½-lb. fully cooked ham slice, ¾ inch thick
- 1 medium green pepper, cut into thin strips
- 1 can (8¾ oz.) apricot halves, drained
- 1 can (8 oz.) pineapple chunks in juice, drained (reserve ¼ cup juice)
- ½ cup sweet and sour sauce
- 1 tablespoon packed brown sugar
- Dash ground cinnamon

4 servings

Place ham slice in 10-inch square baking dish. Arrange green pepper, apricots and pineapple chunks on ham. Set aside. In small bowl, combine reserved pineapple juice, sweet and sour sauce, brown sugar and cinnamon. Pour over ham. Cover. Microwave at 70% (Medium High) for 14 to 17 minutes, or until ham is heated through and green pepper is tender-crisp, rotating dish once.

To reheat: Place one serving on plate. Cover with wax paper. Microwave at 70% (Medium High) for 3 to 4 minutes, or until heated through.

Fruited Ham Slice
Scalloped Potatoes
Buttered Broccoli & Cauliflower Medley
Oatmeal Raisin Cookies

Confetti Ham Casserole

- 1¼ cups hot water
- ⅓ cup finely chopped carrot
- 1½ cups cubed fully cooked ham, ½-inch cubes
- 1 pkg. (4.5 oz.) noodles and Parmesan cheese sauce mix
- ½ cup cubed zucchini, ¼-inch cubes
- ½ cup frozen cut green beans
- ⅓ cup milk
- 2 tablespoons butter or margarine (optional)

Topping:
- 2 teaspoons butter or margarine
- 3 tablespoons seasoned dry bread crumbs
- ½ teaspoon dried parsley flakes

4 to 6 servings

Confetti Ham Casserole
Waldorf Salad
Croissants
Chocolate Chip Cookies

How to Microwave Confetti Ham Casserole

Combine water and carrot in 1½-quart casserole. Cover. Microwave at High for 4½ to 6 minutes, or until water boils. Add remaining ingredients, except topping. Mix well. Re-cover. Microwave at High for 9 to 15 minutes, or just until noodles are tender, stirring 2 or 3 times. Set aside.

Place 2 teaspoons butter in small bowl. Microwave at High for 30 to 45 seconds, or until butter melts. Stir in bread crumbs and parsley. Microwave at High for 30 seconds.

Spread topping evenly over ham and noodle mixture. Microwave, uncovered, at High for 30 seconds.

Italian Chowder

- ¾ lb. Italian sausage links, cut into ½-inch pieces
- 1 can (28 oz.) pear-shaped whole tomatoes, cut up
- ½ cup water
- ¼ cup coarsely chopped onion
- 2 teaspoons sugar
- ½ teaspoon Italian seasoning
- ½ teaspoon salt
- ⅛ teaspoon instant minced garlic
- 1 cup uncooked spiral macaroni
- 1 can (16 oz.) Great Northern beans, drained
- 1 cup frozen broccoli cuts

4 to 6 servings

Place sausage pieces in 3-quart casserole. Microwave at High for 4 to 7 minutes, or until sausage is no longer pink, stirring once. Drain. Stir in tomatoes, water, onion, sugar, Italian seasoning, salt and garlic. Cover. Microwave at High for 5 to 6 minutes, or until bubbly. Stir in macaroni. Re-cover. Microwave at High for 14 to 18 minutes, or until macaroni is tender, stirring once. Stir in beans and broccoli. Re-cover. Microwave at High for 5 to 7 minutes, or until broccoli is tender. Sprinkle each serving with Parmesan cheese, if desired.

To reheat: Place one serving in bowl. Cover with wax paper. Microwave at High for 2 to 3 minutes, or until heated through, stirring once.

Pizza Bake ▲

- 2 cups uncooked egg noodles
- ½ lb. bulk mild Italian sausage
- ½ cup chopped onion
- ¼ cup chopped green pepper
- 1 can (15 oz.) pizza sauce
- ½ cup coarsely chopped pepperoni
- ¼ cup sliced black olives
- 1 cup shredded mozzarella cheese

4 servings

Prepare noodles as directed on package. Rinse and drain. Set aside. Crumble sausage into 1½-quart casserole. Stir in onion and green pepper. Cover. Microwave at High for 5 to 7 minutes, or until sausage is no longer pink, stirring once to break apart. Drain. Combine sausage mixture, noodles and remaining ingredients, except cheese. Re-cover. Microwave at High for 6 to 8 minutes, or until heated through and flavors are blended, stirring once. Sprinkle cheese over casserole. Microwave, uncovered, at High for 2 to 3 minutes, or until cheese melts, rotating casserole once.

To reheat: Place one serving on plate. Cover with wax paper. Microwave at High for 2½ to 4 minutes, or until heated through, stirring once.

Pizza Bake
Lettuce & Tomato Salad with Oil & Vinegar Dressing
Sherbet on Melon Wedges

Italian Chowder
Marinated Mushrooms & Onions in Lemon & Olive Oil Dressing
Cheesy Garlic Bread
Spumoni Ice Cream

Sausage & Mushroom-Rice Bake

- 1 pkg. (8 oz.) fully cooked sausage links
- 1 pkg. (4.4 oz.) mushroom-flavored rice and sauce mix
- 1½ cups hot water
- 1 pkg. (10 oz.) frozen chopped broccoli
- 1 can (4 oz.) sliced mushrooms, drained

4 servings

Brown sausage conventionally as directed on package. Cut each sausage link into 3 pieces. Set aside. In 2-quart casserole, combine rice and sauce mix, water and broccoli. Cover. Microwave at High for 14 to 18 minutes, or until rice is tender and liquid is absorbed, stirring 2 or 3 times to break apart broccoli. Stir in sausage pieces and mushrooms. Re-cover. Microwave at High for 1 minute. Let stand, covered, for 5 minutes.

To reheat: Place one serving on plate. Cover with wax paper. Microwave at High for 2 to 3 minutes, or until heated through, stirring once.

Sausage & Mushroom-Rice Bake
Glazed Acorn Squash   Cloverleaf Dinner Rolls   Cherry Cobbler

◀ Easy Sausage & Cabbage

- 1 pkg. (12 oz.) bulk pork sausage
- 5 cups sliced cabbage, ¼ inch thick
- 1 can (15 oz.) tomato sauce
- ½ cup uncooked instant rice
- ¼ cup sliced green onions
- ½ teaspoon dried crushed sage leaves

4 servings

Crumble sausage into 2-quart casserole. Microwave at High for 4 to 5 minutes, or until sausage is no longer pink, stirring once to break apart. Drain. Mix in remaining ingredients. Cover. Microwave at High for 13 to 18 minutes, or until cabbage is tender-crisp and rice is tender, stirring once.

To reheat: Place one serving on plate. Cover with wax paper. Microwave at High for 2½ to 3½ minutes, or until heated through, stirring once.

Easy Sausage & Cabbage
Mexican Corn
Raisin-Bran Muffins
Vanilla Pudding with Blueberries

Hearty Sausage & Potato Casserole

- 3 cups thinly sliced potatoes (about 1 lb.)
- 1 envelope (1¾ oz.) white sauce mix
- 2 cups milk
- 1 teaspoon dried parsley flakes
- ½ teaspoon caraway seed
- ¼ teaspoon salt
- ⅛ teaspoon pepper
- 1 can (8 oz.) sauerkraut, rinsed and drained
- 1 to 1½ lbs. fully cooked Polish sausages

4 to 6 servings

In 2-quart casserole, combine potatoes, sauce mix, milk, parsley, caraway, salt and pepper. Cover. Microwave at High for 15 to 22 minutes, or until potatoes are tender and sauce thickens, stirring 4 or 5 times. Stir in sauerkraut. Arrange sausages over potato mixture. Re-cover. Microwave at High for 4 to 7 minutes, or until sausages are hot, rotating casserole once. Let stand, covered, for 5 minutes.

To reheat: Place one serving on plate. Cover with wax paper. Microwave at High for 2 to 3 minutes, or until heated through.

Hearty Sausage & Potato Casserole
Broccoli with Sunflower Nuts   Bratwurst Buns   Carrot Cake

Pork Enchiladas

- 1 lb. ground pork
- ⅓ cup chopped onion
- 1 can (10 oz.) enchilada sauce, divided
- 2 tablespoons canned chopped green chilies
- ½ teaspoon ground cumin
- 6 corn tortillas, 6-inch
- 1 cup shredded Cheddar cheese
- 2 tablespoons sliced green onion

4 to 6 servings

Crumble pork into 1½-quart casserole. Add chopped onion. Cover. Microwave at High for 5 to 7 minutes, or until pork is no longer pink, stirring twice to break apart. Drain. Stir in ¼ cup enchilada sauce, the chilies and cumin. Set aside.

Soften tortillas conventionally as directed on package. Place one-sixth of pork mixture in center of each tortilla. Roll up, enclosing filling. Arrange enchiladas seam-side down in 9-inch square baking dish. Pour remaining enchilada sauce over enchiladas. Sprinkle with cheese and sliced green onion. Microwave at 70% (Medium High) for 5 to 7 minutes, or until heated through and cheese melts, rotating dish once or twice.

To reheat: Place one serving on plate. Microwave at 70% (Medium High) for 2 to 3 minutes, or until heated through.

Pork Enchiladas
Refried Beans   Zucchini with Oregano
Glazed Pineapple Slices

Poultry

Chicken with Sausage & Apple Stuffing

- ½ lb. bulk pork sausage
- 1 medium cooking apple, cored and chopped
- ¾ cup onion-garlic croutons
- 2½ to 3-lb. whole broiler-fryer chicken
- 2 tablespoons butter or margarine
- 1 tablespoon dark corn syrup
- ¼ teaspoon bouquet sauce

4 servings

Crumble sausage into 1-quart casserole. Microwave at High for 2½ to 4½ minutes, or until sausage is no longer pink, stirring once to break apart. Drain. Mix sausage, apple and croutons. Fill cavity of chicken with stuffing. Secure legs together with string. Place butter in small bowl. Microwave at High for 45 seconds to 1 minute, or until butter melts. Blend syrup and bouquet sauce into butter.

Place chicken breast-side up on roasting rack. Brush with half of butter mixture. Cover with wax paper. Microwave at 70% (Medium High) for 15 minutes. Rotate rack half turn. Brush with remaining butter mixture. Re-cover. Microwave at 70% (Medium High) for 13 to 20 minutes, or until legs move freely and juices run clear, rotating rack once. Let stand, covered, for 10 minutes.

Chicken with Sausage & Apple Stuffing
Broccoli with Cheese Sauce
Carrot-Raisin Salad
Spice Cookies

Family Favorite Chicken

- 1¼ cups finely crushed buttery round crackers
- 2 teaspoons dried parsley flakes
- ¾ teaspoon seasoned salt
- ½ teaspoon poultry seasoning (optional)
- ¼ teaspoon pepper
- 2 eggs, beaten
- 1 tablespoon vegetable oil
- 2½ to 3-lb. broiler-fryer chicken, cut into 8 pieces, skin removed

4 servings

On sheet of wax paper, combine crackers, parsley, seasoned salt, poultry seasoning and pepper. Set aside. In 9-inch pie plate, blend eggs and oil. Dip chicken into egg mixture, then roll in cracker mixture, pressing lightly to coat. Arrange chicken bone-side down on roasting rack. Cover with paper towel. Microwave at High for 8 minutes. Rearrange chicken. Do not turn chicken over. Re-cover. Microwave at High for 5 to 10 minutes, or until chicken near bone is no longer pink and juices run clear. Let stand, covered, for 3 minutes.

Family Favorite Chicken
Au Gratin Potatoes
Wilted Lettuce Salad
Dinner Rolls
Lemon Bars

Easy Hungarian Chicken

- ½ cup sliced carrot, ¼ inch thick
- 1 pkg. (6¾ oz.) noodles, vegetables and chicken-flavored sauce mix
- 2½ cups hot water
- 1 small green pepper, cut into 1½ × ½-inch strips
- 2½ to 3-lb. broiler-fryer chicken, cut into 8 pieces, skin removed
- 2 teaspoons paprika
- 1 can (16 oz.) stewed tomatoes

4 servings

Place carrot in 3-quart casserole. Cover. Microwave at High for 3 minutes. Stir in noodles and seasoning packet, water and green pepper. Arrange chicken over noodles. Sprinkle evenly with paprika. Pour tomatoes over chicken and noodles. Re-cover. Microwave at High for 25 to 30 minutes, or until chicken near bone is no longer pink and juices run clear, stirring noodles and rearranging chicken twice. Let stand, covered, for 5 to 10 minutes. Serve in shallow bowls. Top with dairy sour cream, if desired.

To reheat: Place one serving in shallow bowl. Cover with wax paper. Microwave at High for 3½ to 4½ minutes, or until heated through.

Easy Hungarian Chicken
Romaine, Cucumber & Red Onion Salad with Sour Cream Dressing
Rye Bread   Apple Strudel

Country-style Chicken

- 2 medium baking potatoes, quartered
- 1 medium yam or sweet potato, peeled and cut into 1-inch pieces
- 1 medium onion, cut into 8 pieces
- ⅔ cup ready-to-serve chicken broth, divided
- 2½ to 3-lb. broiler-fryer chicken, cut into 8 pieces, skin removed
- 2 tablespoons snipped fresh parsley
- ½ teaspoon salt
- ¼ teaspoon dried marjoram leaves
- ¼ teaspoon dried thyme leaves
- ¼ teaspoon pepper

Gravy:

- 3 tablespoons all-purpose flour
- ½ cup milk
- ½ teaspoon bouquet sauce

4 servings

Country-style Chicken
Romaine Salad with Radish Slices
Buttermilk Biscuits
Lemon Meringue Pie

How to Microwave Country-style Chicken

Combine baking potatoes, yams, onion and ⅓ cup broth in 10-inch square casserole. Cover. Microwave at High for 7 to 10 minutes, or just until vegetables are tender, stirring once.

Arrange chicken over vegetables. Combine parsley, salt, marjoram, thyme and pepper with remaining ⅓ cup broth. Pour over chicken. Re-cover.

Microwave at 70% (Medium High) for 22 to 27 minutes, or until chicken near bone is no longer pink and juices run clear, rearranging chicken twice.

Lift chicken and vegetables with slotted spoon to platter. Cover. Set aside. Strain cooking liquid into 4-cup measure. Skim fat, if desired.

Add water to equal 1 cup. In small bowl, blend flour, milk and bouquet sauce with whisk. Blend into cooking liquid.

Microwave at High for 4 to 6 minutes, or until mixture thickens and bubbles, stirring 2 or 3 times with whisk. Serve with chicken and vegetables.

Quick Chicken & Rice

- 1 pkg. (4.6 oz.) rice and sauce mix with peas
- 1⅓ cups hot water
- 1 cup frozen cut green beans
- 2½ to 3-lb. broiler-fryer chicken, cut into 8 pieces, skin removed
- 2 teaspoons dried parsley flakes
- ½ teaspoon paprika
- ¼ teaspoon seasoned salt
- ⅛ teaspoon pepper

4 servings

In 10-inch square casserole, combine rice and sauce mix, water and green beans. Mix well. Arrange chicken over rice mixture. In small bowl, combine parsley, paprika, seasoned salt and pepper. Sprinkle evenly on chicken. Cover. Microwave at High for 15 to 20 minutes, or until chicken near bone is no longer pink and juices run clear, rearranging chicken once or twice. Let stand, covered, for 5 to 10 minutes.

To reheat: Place one serving on plate. Cover with wax paper. Microwave at High for 2½ to 3½ minutes, or until heated through.

Quick Chicken & Rice
Leaf Lettuce with Pineapple Chunks
Crescent Rolls   Raspberry Pie

Creamy Chicken & Vegetables

- 1 pkg. (16 oz.) frozen broccoli cuts with cauliflower
- 2 bone-in whole chicken breasts (10 to 12 oz. each) split in half, skin removed
- ½ teaspoon onion powder
  Seasoned salt (optional)
- 1 can (10¾ oz.) condensed cream of mushroom soup
- ½ cup dairy sour cream
- 1 teaspoon dried parsley flakes
- ¼ teaspoon dried thyme leaves
- 2 tablespoons butter or margarine
- ⅓ cup finely crushed cheese crackers

4 servings

Arrange vegetables in 9-inch square baking dish. Place chicken breast halves over vegetables. Sprinkle with onion powder and seasoned salt. Cover with plastic wrap. Microwave at High for 15 to 20 minutes, or until chicken near bone is no longer pink and juices run clear. Drain. In small mixing bowl, combine soup, sour cream, parsley and thyme. Mix well. Spoon evenly over chicken and vegetables. Re-cover. Microwave at High for 3 to 5 minutes, or until mixture is hot. Place butter in small bowl. Microwave at High for 45 seconds to 1 minute, or until butter melts. Stir in cracker crumbs. Sprinkle evenly over chicken. Microwave, uncovered, at High for 1 minute.

To reheat: Place one serving on plate. Cover with wax paper. Microwave at High for 2 to 3½ minutes, or until heated through.

Creamy Chicken & Vegetables
Herb Bread Stuffing with Walnuts
Sliced Tomatoes
Pudding with Whipped Topping

One-Dish Chicken Teriyaki

- 8 chicken legs (3 to 4 oz. each)
- ½ cup teriyaki sauce
- 1¼ cups hot water
- 1 tablespoon honey
- 1 pkg. (7 oz.) fried rice mix with vermicelli
- 1 pkg. (9 oz.) frozen Italian green beans

4 servings

Place chicken in large plastic food storage bag. Pour teriyaki sauce over chicken. Secure bag. Marinate at room temperature for 15 minutes. Remove chicken from marinade. Set aside.

Reserve 2 tablespoons of marinade. In 2-cup measure, combine water, reserved marinade, honey and seasoning packet from mix. In 10-inch square casserole, combine rice and water mixture. Mix well. Break green beans apart. Stir into rice. Arrange chicken over rice with thickest portions toward outside of casserole. Cover. Microwave at High for 15 to 20 minutes, or until chicken near bone is no longer pink and juices run clear, rotating once or twice.

To reheat: Place one serving on plate. Cover with wax paper. Microwave at 70% (Medium High) for 3 to 4½ minutes, or until heated through.

One-Dish Chicken Teriyaki
Melon & Pineapple Chunks with Honey Dressing
Custard with Whipped Topping

Quick & Easy Chicken Cacciatore ▲

- 8 chicken thighs (4 to 5 oz. each) skin removed
- ½ teaspoon dried oregano leaves
- 1 medium green pepper, thinly sliced
- 1 jar (15½ oz.) spaghetti sauce
- 1 pkg. (4 oz.) shredded mozzarella cheese

4 servings

Arrange chicken in 10-inch square casserole. Sprinkle with oregano. Cover. Microwave at High for 7 to 10 minutes, or until chicken near bone is no longer pink and juices run clear, rearranging chicken after half the time. Drain. Arrange green pepper over chicken. Spoon spaghetti sauce evenly over chicken. Microwave, uncovered, at 70% (Medium High) for 9 to 12 minutes, or until sauce is hot and green pepper is tender-crisp. Sprinkle evenly with cheese. Microwave at 70% (Medium High) for 1 to 2 minutes, or until cheese melts.

To reheat: Place one serving on plate. Cover with wax paper. Microwave at High for 1½ to 3 minutes, or until heated through.

Quick & Easy Chicken Cacciatore
Fettuccine
Lettuce, Green Pepper & Sliced Mushroom Salad
Vanilla Ice Cream with Fudge Sauce

Oriental Chicken & Vegetables

1½ lbs. boneless whole chicken breasts, skin removed, cut into ½-inch strips
2 tablespoons soy sauce
1 tablespoon plus 1 teaspoon cornstarch
2 teaspoons sugar
½ teaspoon ground ginger
½ teaspoon instant chicken bouillon granules
½ cup water
3 cups frozen Oriental vegetable medley
½ to 1 cup shredded lettuce

4 servings

Oriental Chicken & Vegetables
White Rice or Crisp Noodles
Mandarin Oranges & Pineapple Slices on Lettuce
Date Bars

How to Microwave Oriental Chicken & Vegetables

Combine chicken strips and soy sauce in 2-quart casserole. Toss to coat. Cover. Microwave at High for 5 to 8 minutes, or until chicken is no longer pink, stirring once or twice.

Mix cornstarch, sugar, ginger and bouillon in small bowl. Blend in water. Add cornstarch mixture and vegetables to chicken. Re-cover.

Microwave at High for 10 to 16 minutes, or until sauce is thickened and translucent, stirring twice. Stir in lettuce. Let stand, covered, for 1 minute.

Chicken Tetrazzini

- 1 pkg. (7 oz.) vermicelli
- 4 slices bacon, cut up
- 2 tablespoons all-purpose flour
- ¼ teaspoon salt
- ¼ teaspoon dried basil leaves
- ⅛ teaspoon pepper
- 1⅓ cups milk
- ¼ cup sliced green onions
- 1½ cups shredded pasteurized process American cheese
- 2 cups cut-up cooked chicken or turkey
- 1 can (4 oz.) sliced mushrooms, drained

6 servings

Prepare vermicelli as directed on package. Rinse and drain. Set aside. Place bacon in 2-quart casserole. Microwave at High for 4 to 6 minutes, or until brown and crisp, stirring once. Remove bacon with slotted spoon to paper towel. Set aside.

Reserve 2 tablespoons bacon fat in casserole. Stir in flour, salt, basil and pepper. Blend in milk. Stir in onions. Microwave at High for 5 to 7 minutes, or until mixture thickens and bubbles, stirring twice.

Stir in cheese until melted. Add chicken, mushrooms and vermicelli. Mix well. Microwave at High for 5 to 7 minutes, or until heated through, stirring once. Sprinkle with bacon.

To reheat: Place one serving on plate. Cover with wax paper. Microwave at High for 1½ to 2½ minutes, or until heated through.

Chicken Tetrazzini
Buttered Broccoli Spears with Italian Seasoning
Bread Sticks or Garlic Bread
Chocolate Cake

Chicken & Spinach Rice

- 1 pkg. (10 oz.) frozen chopped spinach
- 3 tablespoons butter or margarine, divided
- 1 pkg. (8 oz.) chicken-flavored rice and vermicelli mix (reserve seasoning packet)
- 3 cups hot water
- ½ teaspoon poultry seasoning
- ¼ teaspoon pepper
- 2 cups cut-up cooked chicken
- 1 can (8 oz.) sliced water chestnuts, drained
- ⅓ cup sliced almonds

4 to 6 servings

Unwrap spinach and place on plate. Microwave at High for 4 to 6 minutes, or until defrosted. Drain thoroughly, pressing to remove excess moisture. Set aside. In 2-quart casserole, combine 2 tablespoons butter and rice and vermicelli. Microwave at High for 4 to 6 minutes, or until vermicelli is light brown, stirring 2 or 3 times. Stir in water, seasoning packet, poultry seasoning and pepper. Cover. Microwave at High for 5 to 10 minutes, or until mixture starts to thicken and liquid is partially absorbed, stirring once. Stir in chicken, spinach and water chestnuts. Re-cover. Microwave at High for 6 to 8 minutes, or until rice is tender. Set aside.

Place almonds and remaining 1 tablespoon butter in 9-inch pie plate. Microwave at High for 4 to 6 minutes, or until light golden brown, stirring twice. Sprinkle over top of casserole.

To reheat: Place one serving on plate. Cover with wax paper. Microwave at High for 1½ to 3 minutes, or until heated through, stirring once.

Chicken & Spinach Rice
Cottage Cheese-filled Pear Halves
Sesame Seed Bread Sticks
Orange Crisp Cookies

Individual Chicken Stew with Dumplings

- 1 can (4.5 oz.) refrigerated buttermilk biscuits
- 2 tablespoons butter or margarine
- ⅓ cup cornflake crumbs
- 1 pkg. (2⅝ oz.) instant cream-style chicken soup mix
- 3 cups hot water
- 2 cups cut-up cooked chicken
- 2 cups frozen mixed vegetables

4 servings

Individual Chicken Stew with Dumplings
Cherry Gelatin Mold with Fruit Cocktail
Chocolate Chip Cookies

How to Microwave Individual Chicken Stew with Dumplings

Separate biscuits. Cut each biscuit in half. Place butter in small bowl. Microwave at High for 45 seconds to 1 minute, or until butter melts. Place cornflake crumbs on sheet of wax paper. Dip each biscuit half in butter, then roll in crumbs. Set aside.

Place contents of one envelope of soup mix and ¾ cup water in each 15-oz. bowl. Mix well. Divide chicken and vegetables among bowls. Arrange bowls in microwave oven. Microwave at High for 14 to 18 minutes, or until mixture thickens, stirring after every 4 minutes.

Top each bowl with 3 biscuit halves. Microwave at High for 3 to 4½ minutes, or until dumplings are firm and cooked through, rotating bowls once.

Easy Sweet & Sour Chicken

- 1 can (11 oz.) mandarin oranges, drained (reserve ¼ cup syrup)
- 1 can (8¼ oz.) pineapple chunks in heavy syrup, drained (reserve ¼ cup syrup)
- 1 envelope (2 oz.) sweet and sour sauce mix
- ¼ cup vinegar
- 1 medium tomato, seeded and chopped
- ½ cup green pepper pieces, 1-inch pieces
- 1 pkg. (12 oz.) frozen breaded chicken chunks

4 to 6 servings

In 2-quart casserole, combine orange and pineapple syrups. Add sauce mix and vinegar. Mix well. Stir in tomato. Microwave at High for 6 to 8 minutes, or until sauce is thickened and translucent, stirring twice. Stir in green pepper and chicken. Microwave at High for 5 to 8 minutes, or until chicken is heated through, stirring once. Gently stir in oranges and pineapple. Microwave at High for 1 to 2 minutes, or until heated through. Let stand, covered, for 3 minutes.

Easy Sweet & Sour Chicken
White Rice
Spinach & Bean Sprout Salad with Toasted Sesame Seed Dressing
Almond or Fortune Cookies

Herb-seasoned Cornish Hens ▲

- 2 teaspoons Italian seasoning
- 1 teaspoon salt
- ¼ teaspoon pepper
- ⅛ teaspoon garlic powder
- 4 Cornish hens (18 oz. each)
- 1 cup chopped onions
- ¼ cup butter or margarine

4 servings

In small bowl, combine Italian seasoning, salt, pepper and garlic powder. Sprinkle cavity of each Cornish hen with ¼ teaspoon seasoning mixture. Reserve remaining mixture. Fill each cavity with ¼ cup onions. Secure legs together with string. Arrange Cornish hens breast-side up on roasting rack. Place butter in 1-cup measure. Microwave at High for 1¼ to 1½ minutes, or until butter melts. Add reserved seasoning mixture to butter. Brush butter mixture on hens. Cover with wax paper. Microwave at High for 22 to 32 minutes, or until legs move freely and juices run clear, brushing with butter mixture and rotating rack twice. Let stand, covered, for 5 minutes.

To reheat: Place one serving on plate. Cover with wax paper. Microwave at 70% (Medium High) for 3 to 4 minutes, or until heated through.

Herb-seasoned Cornish Hens
White & Wild Rice with Mushrooms
Italian Green Beans with Lemon Butter   Orange Sherbet

Apricot-glazed Turkey ▶

- 4-lb. boneless whole turkey
- ½ teaspoon dried marjoram leaves
- ¼ teaspoon pepper
- 1 jar (12 oz.) apricot preserves
- 1 tablespoon butter or margarine

6 to 8 servings

Apricot-glazed Turkey
Baked Potatoes with Butter & Sour Cream
Buttered Asparagus with Sunflower Nuts
Lettuce, Cauliflowerets & Carrot Salad
Pineapple Sherbet

How to Microwave Apricot-glazed Turkey

Place turkey on roasting rack. Rub with marjoram and pepper. Cover with wax paper. Microwave at High for 10 minutes.

Combine apricot preserves and butter in 2-cup measure. Microwave at High for 1 to 2 minutes, or until mixture bubbles. Brush all sides of turkey with one-third of apricot mixture. Re-cover.

Microwave at 70% (Medium High) for 35 to 45 minutes, or until internal temperature registers 175°F, in several places, turning turkey over and brushing once with apricot mixture. Let stand, tented with foil, for 10 minutes.

Savory Italian Turkey ▲

3 to 4-lb. bone-in turkey breast half	½ teaspoon dried oregano leaves
¾ cup Italian dressing	¼ teaspoon dried rosemary leaves

6 to 8 servings

Place turkey in large plastic food storage bag. In 1-cup measure, combine Italian dressing, oregano and rosemary. Pour over turkey. Secure bag. Place bag on plate. Refrigerate for at least 8 hours or overnight, turning bag over once.

Remove turkey from marinade. Discard marinade. Place turkey skin-side down on roasting rack. Cover with wax paper. Microwave at High for 10 minutes. Turn turkey skin-side up. Re-cover. Microwave at 50% (Medium) for 30 to 45 minutes, or until internal temperature registers 170°F in thickest portion. Let stand, tented with foil, for 10 minutes.

To reheat: Place one serving on plate. Cover with wax paper. Microwave at 70% (Medium High) for 1½ to 2 minutes, or until heated through.

Place remaining apricot mixture in small bowl. Microwave at High for 1 to 1½ minutes, or until heated through. Serve with sliced turkey.

Savory Italian Turkey		
Parmesan Noodles	Antipasto Tray	Cherry Cheesecake

Family Favorites/Poultry

Creole-sauced Turkey

- 1 can (8 oz.) stewed tomatoes
- ½ cup sliced green onions
- ½ cup catsup
- 1 tablespoon packed brown sugar
- 1 tablespoon vinegar
- ½ teaspoon dry mustard
- ½ teaspoon dried thyme leaves
- ¼ teaspoon salt
- 2 turkey tenderloins (about ¾ lb. each)

6 servings

In 10-inch square casserole, combine all ingredients, except turkey. Mix well. Place turkey in tomato mixture. Spoon sauce over turkey. Cover. Microwave at High for 5 minutes. Spoon sauce over turkey. Re-cover. Microwave at 70% (Medium High) for 16 to 22 minutes, or until turkey is firm and no longer pink, rotating casserole once. Let stand, covered, for 5 to 10 minutes.

To reheat: Place one serving on plate. Cover with wax paper. Microwave at 70% (Medium High) for 1½ to 2 minutes, or until heated through.

Creole-sauced Turkey
White Rice or Egg Noodles   Green & Red Pepper Slices
Butterscotch Brownies

Mustard Turkey Slices

- 1 cup dairy sour cream
- 1 tablespoon Dijon or prepared mustard
- 2 teaspoons lemon juice
- 1 teaspoon honey
- ¼ teaspoon salt
- ¾ cup cornflake crumbs
- ½ teaspoon paprika
- ⅛ teaspoon garlic powder
- 1 to 1½ lbs. turkey tenderloins, diagonally sliced ½ inch thick
- ½ teaspoon dried parsley flakes

4 to 6 servings

In shallow bowl, blend sour cream, mustard, lemon juice, honey and salt. Reserve half of sour cream mixture in small bowl. Set aside. On sheet of wax paper, combine cornflake crumbs, paprika and garlic powder. Dip each turkey slice in sour cream mixture, then roll in cornflake mixture, pressing lightly to coat. Place turkey on roasting rack. Microwave at 70% (Medium High) for 10 minutes. Rearrange turkey slices. Microwave at 70% (Medium High) for 8 to 10 minutes, or until turkey is firm and no longer pink. Combine reserved sour cream mixture and parsley. Microwave at 50% (Medium) for 1½ to 2½ minutes, or until heated through, stirring once. Serve sauce with turkey.

Mustard Turkey Slices
Rice Medley   Buttered Brussels Sprouts
Apple Crisp or Cherry Cobbler

Easy Turkey Loaf ▶

Loaf:
- 4 slices bacon
- 1½ lbs. ground turkey
- ¼ cup unseasoned dry bread crumbs
- ¼ teaspoon salt
- ¼ teaspoon ground nutmeg
- ⅛ teaspoon pepper
- 2 eggs, slightly beaten
- 2 tablespoons milk

Sauce:
- 1 envelope (.87 oz.) white sauce mix
- ½ teaspoon dried parsley flakes
- ⅛ teaspoon ground nutmeg
- 1 cup milk

6 to 8 servings

> **Easy Turkey Loaf**
> Parsleyed New Potatoes
> Marinated Cucumber Salad
> Fruit Compote

How to Microwave Easy Turkey Loaf

Place bacon on roasting rack. Cover with paper towel. Microwave at High for 3 to 5 minutes, or until brown and crisp. Cool slightly. Crumble.

Combine all loaf ingredients in medium mixing bowl. Mix well. Press into 8 × 4-inch loaf dish. Place dish on saucer in microwave oven. Cover with wax paper.

Microwave at High for 5 minutes. Rotate dish half turn. Microwave at 70% (Medium High) for 9 to 13 minutes, or until center of loaf is firm, rotating dish once. Set aside.

Home-style Turkey Hash

- 1 pkg. (12 oz.) frozen hash brown potatoes
- 1 lb. ground turkey
- ½ cup chopped onion
- ½ cup chopped green pepper
- 1 cup chili sauce or catsup
- 1 jar (2 oz.) sliced pimiento, drained
- ½ teaspoon salt
- ¼ teaspoon pepper

4 to 6 servings

Unwrap potatoes and place on plate. Microwave at 50% (Medium) for 1½ to 3 minutes, or until defrosted. Break potatoes into small pieces. Set aside. Crumble turkey into 2-quart casserole. Add onion and green pepper. Cover. Microwave at High for 6 to 8 minutes, or until turkey is firm, stirring once or twice to break apart. Drain. Stir in chili sauce, pimiento, salt and pepper. Stir in potatoes. Microwave, uncovered, at High for 4 to 6 minutes, or until hot, stirring once.

Home-style Turkey Hash
Poached Eggs
Toasted English Muffins
Strawberries & Orange Slices

Combine sauce mix, parsley and nutmeg in 4-cup measure. Blend in milk. Beat with whisk.

Microwave at High for 4 to 6 minutes, or until mixture thickens and bubbles, stirring twice. Serve with loaf.

To reheat: Place one serving on plate. Cover with wax paper. Microwave at 70% (Medium High) for 1½ to 2½ minutes, or until heated through.

Fish & Seafood

◄ Hearty Fish Chowder

- ½ cup chopped green pepper
- ½ cup coarsely chopped onion
- 2 tablespoons olive oil
- 1 can (28 oz.) whole tomatoes, cut up
- 1 cup water
- 1 pkg. (2.8 oz.) minestrone soup mix with pasta
- ¼ teaspoon Italian seasoning
- ½ lb. cod fillets, ¾ inch thick, cut into 1-inch pieces
- 4 seafood sticks (1 oz. each) cut into 1-inch pieces

4 to 6 servings

In 2-quart casserole, combine green pepper, onion and olive oil. Cover. Microwave at High for 2 to 3 minutes, or until vegetables are tender-crisp. Stir in tomatoes, water, soup mix and Italian seasoning. Re-cover. Microwave at High for 20 to 28 minutes, or until pasta is tender, stirring twice. Gently stir in fish and seafood pieces. Re-cover. Microwave at High for 3 to 4 minutes, or until fish flakes easily with fork, stirring once.

To reheat: Place one serving in bowl. Cover with wax paper. Microwave at High for 2 to 3 minutes, or until heated through, stirring once.

Hearty Fish Chowder
French Bread
Coconut Cream Pie

Herb Buttered Fish Fillets ▼

- 1 pkg. (12 oz.) individually wrapped frozen fish fillets*
- ¼ cup butter or margarine
- 1 teaspoon dried parsley flakes
- ½ teaspoon dried dill weed

2 to 4 servings

Arrange frozen fillets in 9-inch square baking dish with thickest portions toward outside of dish. In small bowl, combine butter, parsley and dill. Microwave at High for 1¼ to 1½ minutes, or until butter melts. Pour evenly over fish. Cover with wax paper. Microwave at High for 6 to 9 minutes, or until fish flakes easily with fork, rotating dish once or twice. Let stand, covered, for 3 minutes.

*If fillets cannot be separated, place on plate. Microwave at 50% (Medium) for 1½ to 2 minutes, or until easily separated, but still icy. Unwrap fillets.

To reheat: Place one serving on plate. Cover with wax paper. Microwave at High for 1 to 2 minutes, or until heated through.

Herb Buttered Fish Fillets
Rice Medley   *Sautéed Zucchini*
Butterflake Rolls   *Sugar Cookies*

Fillets with Swiss Cheese Sauce

- ¼ cup butter or margarine, divided
- 2 teaspoons dried parsley flakes, divided
- 1 teaspoon freeze-dried chives, divided
- 1 cup onion-garlic croutons, crushed
- 3 tablespoons all-purpose flour
- ¼ teaspoon salt
- 1 cup milk
- ⅓ cup shredded Swiss cheese
- 1 lb. fish fillets, ½ inch thick, cut into serving-size pieces

4 to 6 servings

In small mixing bowl, combine 2 tablespoons butter, 1 teaspoon parsley and ½ teaspoon chives. Microwave at High for 45 seconds to 1 minute, or until butter melts. Stir in crushed croutons until moistened. Set aside. Place remaining 2 tablespoons butter in 2-cup measure. Microwave at High for 45 seconds to 1 minute, or until butter melts. Stir in flour, remaining 1 teaspoon parsley, remaining ½ teaspoon chives and the salt. Blend in milk. Microwave at High for 3 to 4 minutes, or until mixture thickens and bubbles, stirring well with whisk after every minute. Stir in cheese until melted. Set aside.

Arrange fish in 10-inch square casserole. Pour sauce over fillets. Cover with wax paper. Microwave at High for 4 to 6 minutes, or until fish flakes easily with fork, rearranging fish once. Sprinkle crouton mixture over fish. Microwave, uncovered, at 70% (Medium High) for 2 minutes.

To reheat: Place one serving on plate. Cover with wax paper. Microwave at High for 1½ to 3 minutes, or until heated through.

Fillets with Swiss Cheese Sauce
Peas & Carrots with Grated Lemon Peel
Iceberg & Leaf Lettuce with Oil & Vinegar Dressing
Chocolate Pound Cake with Whipped Topping

Lemony Fillets & Rice

- 1 cup hot water
- ¼ cup sliced green onions
- 2 tablespoons butter or margarine
- 1 tablespoon dried parsley flakes
- 1 tablespoon plus 1 teaspoon lemon juice, divided
- ½ teaspoon instant chicken bouillon granules
- 1 cup uncooked instant rice
- 1 pkg. (12 oz.) individually wrapped frozen fish fillets*
- ¼ teaspoon dried thyme leaves

4 servings

In 10-inch square casserole, combine water, onions, butter, parsley, 1 tablespoon lemon juice and the bouillon. Microwave at High for 4 to 6 minutes, or until water boils. Stir in rice. Arrange frozen fillets on rice with thicker portions toward outside of casserole. Sprinkle remaining 1 teaspoon lemon juice on fish. Sprinkle with thyme. Cover. Microwave at High for 7 to 10 minutes, or until fish flakes easily with fork, rotating casserole once or twice. Fluff rice with fork before serving.

*If fillets cannot be separated, place on plate. Microwave at 50% (Medium) for 1½ to 2 minutes, or until easily separated, but still icy. Unwrap fillets.

To reheat: Place one serving on plate. Cover with wax paper. Microwave at High for 2 to 3½ minutes, or until heated through.

Lemony Fillets & Rice
Green Beans   Whole Wheat Muffins   Cheesecake

Fish in Spicy Red Sauce ▶

- 1 cup coarsely chopped celery
- ½ cup chopped onion
- ½ cup chopped green pepper
- 2 tablespoons butter or margarine
- 1 tablespoon all-purpose flour
- ½ teaspoon dried oregano leaves
- ¼ teaspoon salt
- ¼ teaspoon chili powder
- ⅛ teaspoon pepper
- 1 can (8 oz.) tomato sauce
- 1 can (16 oz.) whole tomatoes, cut up
- ¾ lb. fish fillets, ¾ inch thick, cut into 1-inch pieces

4 servings

Fish in Spicy Red Sauce
Parsley-Buttered Egg Noodles
Peach Halves on Lettuce
Lemon Cookies

How to Microwave Fish in Spicy Red Sauce

Combine celery, onion, green pepper and butter in 2-quart casserole. Cover.

Microwave at High for 3 to 5 minutes, or until vegetables are tender-crisp, stirring once.

Stir in flour, oregano, salt, chili powder and pepper. Blend in tomato sauce. Stir in tomatoes and fish pieces. Re-cover.

Quick Mexican Fish Fillets

1 pkg. (14 oz.) frozen breaded fish fillets	4 oz. Monterey Jack cheese, thinly sliced
3 tablespoons taco sauce	¼ cup canned chopped green chilies, drained

4 to 6 servings

Place 2 paper towels on 12-inch round platter. Arrange frozen fish on paper towel-lined platter. Cover with another paper towel. Microwave at High for 6 to 9 minutes, or until fish is heated through, rotating platter once.

Spread taco sauce lightly on top of each fillet. Top with cheese and green chilies. Microwave, uncovered, at 70% (Medium High) for 2 to 3 minutes, or until cheese melts, rotating platter once.

Microwave at High for 10 to 16 minutes, or until fish flakes easily with fork, stirring twice.

Quick Mexican Fish Fillets
Mexican Corn   Zucchini & Tomato Salad
Shortbread Cookies

Salmon-Rice Chowder

- ½ cup chopped celery
- ¼ cup chopped onion
- 1 tablespoon butter or margarine
- 1 can (12 oz.) evaporated milk
- ¼ teaspoon dried marjoram leaves
- ¼ teaspoon salt
- ⅛ teaspoon pepper
- 1 pkg. (10 oz.) frozen long grain and wild rice
- 1 cup frozen peas and carrots
- 1 can (12½ oz.) skinless, boneless salmon, drained

4 servings

In 2-quart casserole, combine celery, onion and butter. Cover. Microwave at High for 2 to 4 minutes, or until celery is tender-crisp. Stir in evaporated milk, marjoram, salt and pepper. Remove frozen rice from pouch. Add rice to milk mixture. Re-cover. Microwave at High for 7 to 8 minutes, stirring twice to break apart. Stir in peas and carrots. Re-cover. Microwave at High for 5 minutes. Gently stir in salmon. Re-cover. Microwave at High for 5 to 8 minutes, or until heated through and flavors are blended, stirring once.

To reheat: Place one serving in bowl. Cover with wax paper. Microwave at High for 2 to 3 minutes, or until heated through, stirring once.

Salmon-Rice Chowder
Dark Rye Bread   Pound Cake with Peaches & Raspberries

Tuna Pie

- 1 pkg. (9 oz.) frozen cut green beans
- 1 cup cooked rice
- 1 baked 9-inch pastry shell
- 1 can (12½ oz.) tuna, drained
- 1 can (10¾ oz.) condensed cream of mushroom soup
- 2 eggs, slightly beaten
- 1 teaspoon instant minced onion
- ⅛ teaspoon pepper
- ¼ cup shredded Cheddar cheese

6 servings

Unwrap green beans and place on plate. Microwave at High for 3 to 5 minutes, or until defrosted. Drain. Set aside. Spread rice evenly over bottom of pastry shell. Crumble tuna evenly over rice. In medium mixing bowl, combine green beans, soup, eggs, onion and pepper. Mix well. Pour over tuna. Cover with wax paper.

Place pie plate on saucer in microwave oven. Microwave at 70% (Medium High) for 15 to 20 minutes, or until center is set. Sprinkle with cheese. Let stand, covered, for 5 to 8 minutes.

To reheat: Place one serving on plate. Cover with wax paper. Microwave at High for 1½ to 2½ minutes, or until heated through.

Tuna Pie
Sliced Tomatoes
Chocolate Sundaes with Pecans

Salmon-Noodle Casserole

- 1½ cups water
- ½ cup chopped celery
- 2 tablespoons butter or margarine
- 1 pkg. (4.5 oz.) noodles and Italian cheese sauce mix
- 1 small zucchini, cut in half lengthwise, sliced ¼ inch thick
- ½ cup milk
- ¼ teaspoon garlic salt
- ¼ teaspoon pepper
- 1 can (6¾ oz.) skinless, boneless salmon, drained
- 1½ tablespoons butter
- 1 teaspoon parsley flakes
- ½ cup herb seasoned stuffing mix
- Paprika (optional)

4 servings

In 1½-quart casserole, combine water, celery and butter. Cover. Microwave at High for 5 to 8 minutes, or until water boils. Stir in noodles and sauce mix, zucchini, milk, garlic salt and pepper. Microwave, uncovered, at High for 6 to 9 minutes, or until mixture thickens and bubbles, stirring once. Gently stir in salmon. Cover. Set aside. Place butter and parsley in small mixing bowl. Microwave at High for 45 seconds to 1 minute, or until butter melts. Add stuffing. Stir until moistened. Sprinkle evenly over casserole. Sprinkle with paprika. Microwave at High for 1 minute.

Salmon-Noodle Casserole
Romaine & Carrot Curl Salad   Croissants   Brownies

◄ Cheesy Tuna Bake

- 1 pkg. (10 oz.) frozen chopped spinach
- 1 can (7½ oz.) semi-condensed cream of mushroom soup
- 1 cup unseasoned whole wheat and white croutons
- 1 cup shredded Swiss cheese
- 1 can (6½ oz.) tuna, drained
- ½ cup shredded carrot
- ½ teaspoon onion powder

4 servings

Unwrap spinach and place on plate. Microwave at High for 4 to 6 minutes, or until defrosted. Drain thoroughly, pressing to remove excess moisture. In medium mixing bowl, combine spinach and remaining ingredients. Mix well. Spoon mixture into 1-quart casserole. Cover. Microwave at 70% (Medium High) for 7 to 10 minutes, or until hot and cheese melts, stirring once or twice. Sprinkle with paprika, if desired.

Cheesy Tuna Bake
Orange Gelatin Salad on Lettuce
Chocolate Cake

Spanish Tuna Casserole

- ⅓ cup chopped green pepper
- ¼ cup chopped onion
- 1 can (10¾ oz.) condensed creamy asparagus soup
- 1 cup uncooked instant rice
- 1 can (6½ oz.) tuna, drained
- ½ cup milk
- 1 jar (2 oz.) sliced pimiento, drained
- 2 tablespoons chopped black olives
- ½ teaspoon dried basil leaves
- ⅛ teaspoon pepper
- 2 tablespoons grated Parmesan cheese (optional)

4 servings

In 1½-quart casserole, combine green pepper and onion. Cover. Microwave at High for 2 minutes. Stir in remaining ingredients, except cheese. Mix well. Re-cover. Microwave at High for 10 to 13 minutes, or until rice is tender, stirring once. Sprinkle with Parmesan cheese. Let stand, covered, for 5 minutes.

To reheat: Place one serving on plate. Cover with wax paper. Microwave at High for 1½ to 2 minutes, or until heated through.

Spanish Tuna Casserole
Radishes, Carrot Sticks & Black Olives   Dinner Rolls   Lime Sherbet

Crab à la King

- 1 pkg. (10 oz.) frozen mixed vegetables
- 2 tablespoons water
- 1 envelope (.87 oz.) white sauce mix
- ¼ teaspoon Italian seasoning
- 1¼ cups milk
- 1 can (6 oz.) crab meat, rinsed, drained and cartilage removed
- 2 tablespoons grated Parmesan cheese

4 servings

In 1-quart casserole, combine mixed vegetables and water. Cover. Microwave at High for 5 to 8 minutes, or until vegetables are hot, stirring once. Drain. Re-cover. Set aside. In 4-cup measure, combine sauce mix and Italian seasoning. Blend in milk. Beat well with whisk. Microwave at High for 5 to 8 minutes, or until mixture thickens and bubbles, stirring 2 or 3 times. Add sauce and crab to vegetables. Stir. Microwave, uncovered, at High for 1 to 2 minutes, or until hot. Stir in cheese.

To reheat: Place one serving in bowl. Cover with wax paper. Microwave at 70% (Medium High) for 3 to 4 minutes, or until heated through, stirring once.

Crab à la King
Patty Shells or Toast Points
Melon & Blueberry Salad with Poppy Seed-Honey Dressing
Lemon Coconut Cake

Oyster-Broccoli Au Gratin

- 2 cups frozen broccoli cuts
- ¼ cup chopped celery
- ¼ cup chopped onion
- 1 envelope (.87 oz.) white sauce mix
- 1¼ cups milk
- ½ cup shredded Cheddar cheese, divided
- 1 cup crushed saltine crackers
- 2 cans (8 oz. each) oysters, drained

4 servings

Oyster-Broccoli Au Gratin
Leaf Lettuce & Pear Salad
Poppy Seed Bread Sticks
Oatmeal Spice Cookies

How to Microwave Oyster-Broccoli Au Gratin

Combine broccoli, celery and onion in 1-quart casserole. Cover. Microwave at High for 5 to 6 minutes, or until vegetables are tender, stirring once. Drain. Set aside.

Place sauce mix in 4-cup measure. Blend in milk. Beat well with whisk. Microwave at High for 5 to 8 minutes, or until mixture thickens and bubbles, stirring 2 or 3 times. Stir in ¼ cup cheese until melted. Set aside.

Layer half of crushed crackers, the oysters and vegetables in 1½-quart casserole. Pour sauce over vegetable layer. Sprinkle with remaining crushed crackers and remaining ¼ cup cheese. Microwave at High for 5 to 9 minutes, or until heated through and bubbly around edges, rotating casserole once.

Spicy Shrimp Bake

½ cup chopped onion
½ cup chopped green pepper
1⅓ cups uncooked instant rice
1 can (16 oz.) whole tomatoes, cut up
1 can (8 oz.) tomato sauce
½ teaspoon garlic salt
⅛ teaspoon hot pepper sauce
1½ cups cubed pasteurized process cheese spread with jalapeño peppers, 1-inch cubes
1 can (4¼ oz.) large shrimp, rinsed and drained

4 to 6 servings

In 1½-quart casserole, combine onion and green pepper. Cover. Microwave at High for 3 to 4 minutes, or until vegetables are tender, stirring once. Stir in rice, tomatoes, tomato sauce, garlic salt and hot pepper sauce. Re-cover. Microwave at High for 10 to 13 minutes, or until rice is tender, stirring once. Stir in cheese. Re-cover. Microwave at High for 2 to 3 minutes, or until cheese melts and can be stirred smooth, stirring once. Gently stir in shrimp. Let stand, covered, for 5 minutes.

To reheat: Place one serving on plate. Cover with wax paper. Microwave at High for 1½ to 2½ minutes, or until heated through, stirring once.

Spicy Shrimp Bake
Cucumber & Carrots in Lime Gelatin
French Bread
Banana Nut Cake

Creamy Clam Chowder ▲

2 slices bacon, cut up
¼ cup chopped onion
2 cans (10¾ oz. each) condensed creamy potato soup
2 cans (6½ oz. each) minced clams, undrained
½ cup milk
1 tablespoon dried parsley flakes

4 servings

In 2-quart casserole, combine bacon and onion. Cover. Microwave at High for 4 to 6 minutes, or until onion is tender-crisp, stirring once. Stir in remaining ingredients. Mix well. Re-cover. Microwave at High for 8 to 10 minutes, or until heated through, stirring once.

To reheat: Place one serving in bowl. Cover with wax paper. Microwave at High for 2 to 4 minutes, or until heated through, stirring once or twice.

Creamy Clam Chowder
Cheese Biscuits   Strawberry-Rhubarb Crisp

Family Favorites/Fish & Seafood

Meatless

Individual Spinach Stratas

- 1 pkg. (10 oz.) frozen chopped spinach
- 4 slices white bread
- 1 pkg. (6 oz.) shredded Swiss cheese
- 6 eggs, slightly beaten
- ⅔ cup half-and-half
- 2 teaspoons instant minced onion
- ½ teaspoon seasoned salt
- ⅛ teaspoon pepper

4 servings

Individual Spinach Stratas
Fresh Fruit Salad
Croissants
Lemon Pudding with Whipped Topping

How to Microwave Individual Spinach Stratas

Unwrap spinach and place on plate. Microwave at High for 4 to 6 minutes, or until defrosted. Drain thoroughly, pressing to remove excess moisture.

Place one slice of bread in bottom of four (14 oz. each) square individual casseroles. Top each with 3 tablespoons cheese, one-fourth of spinach and another 3 tablespoons cheese. Set aside.

Combine remaining ingredients in 4-cup measure. Mix well. Pour ½ cup of egg mixture evenly into each casserole. Cover with plastic wrap. Refrigerate for 4 hours or overnight. Remove plastic wrap.

Cover with wax paper. Arrange casseroles in microwave oven.

Microwave at 70% (Medium High) for 15 to 20 minutes, or until centers are puffed and set, rearranging after every 5 minutes.

Family Favorites/Meatless 81

Cheesy Chili-stuffed Tortillas ▲

- 1 can (7 oz.) whole green chilies, drained
- 2 oz. Monterey Jack cheese, thinly sliced
- 1½ cups shredded Cheddar cheese, divided
- 1 cup small curd cottage cheese
- ½ teaspoon ground cumin
- ¼ teaspoon garlic salt
- ¼ teaspoon dried oregano leaves
- 4 flour tortillas, 8-inch
- 1 envelope (.87 oz.) white sauce mix
- 1 cup milk

4 servings

Cheesy Chili-stuffed Tortillas
Refried Beans
Avocado & Orange Slices on Leaf Lettuce
Snickerdoodle Cookies

How to Microwave Cheesy Chili-stuffed Tortillas

Place chilies on paper towels. Cut lengthwise slit in each chili. Remove seeds. Cut Monterey Jack cheese to fit inside each chili. Set aside.

Combine 1 cup Cheddar cheese, the cottage cheese, cumin, garlic salt and oregano in small mixing bowl. Mix well. Place one-fourth of cheese mixture down center of each flour tortilla.

82 Family Favorites/Meatless

Deluxe Macaroni & Cheese ▶

- 1 pkg. (7 oz.) elbow macaroni
- 2 cups small curd cottage cheese
- 2 cups shredded sharp Cheddar cheese
- 1 cup dairy sour cream
- 1 egg, slightly beaten
- ½ teaspoon salt
- ⅛ teaspoon pepper
- Paprika

6 to 8 servings

Prepare macaroni as directed on package. Rinse and drain. In 2-quart casserole, combine macaroni and remaining ingredients, except paprika. Mix well. Cover. Microwave at 70% (Medium High) for 9 to 12 minutes, or until heated through and cheese melts, stirring twice. Sprinkle with paprika.

To reheat: Place one serving on plate. Cover with wax paper. Microwave at High for 1½ to 2½ minutes, or until heated through, stirring once.

Deluxe Macaroni & Cheese
Carrot & Celery Sticks   Garlic Toast   Mint Brownies

Arrange stuffed chili over cheese mixture. Roll up, enclosing cheese mixture and stuffed chili. Place stuffed tortillas seam-side down in 9-inch square baking dish. Set aside.

Place sauce mix in 2-cup measure. Blend in milk. Beat well with whisk. Microwave at High for 4 to 6 minutes, or until mixture thickens and bubbles, stirring with whisk 2 or 3 times.

Pour sauce evenly over tortillas. Sprinkle with remaining ½ cup Cheddar cheese. Microwave at 70% (Medium High) for 12 to 15 minutes, or until centers are heated through and cheese melts, rotating dish once or twice.

◀ Double Cheese Linguine

- 1 pkg. (7 oz.) linguine
- 1 cup chopped zucchini
- 1 cup frozen peas
- 3 tablespoons butter or margarine
- 3 eggs
- ¼ cup half-and-half
- ¼ teaspoon salt
- 1 cup finely shredded mozzarella cheese
- ½ cup grated Parmesan cheese

4 servings

Prepare linguine as directed on package. Rinse and drain. Set aside. In 2-quart casserole, combine zucchini, peas and butter. Cover. Microwave at High for 4 to 6 minutes, or until vegetables are tender-crisp, stirring once. Set aside.

In small mixing bowl, blend eggs, half-and-half and salt. Add egg mixture, linguine, mozzarella and Parmesan cheeses to vegetable mixture. Toss to coat. Microwave, uncovered, at High for 6 to 8 minutes, or until mixture is set, tossing after every 2 minutes. Sprinkle with freshly ground pepper, if desired.

To reheat: Place one serving on plate. Cover with wax paper. Microwave at High for 2 to 3 minutes, or until heated through.

Double Cheese Linguine
Tomato Wedges with Italian Dressing
Hard Rolls
Raspberry Frozen Yogurt

Cheese Grits

- 1½ cups hot water
- ½ cup uncooked quick-cooking grits
- ¼ teaspoon salt
- ⅓ cup half-and-half
- 2 eggs
- 2 cups shredded Cheddar cheese
- ½ cup seeded chopped tomato
- 2 tablespoons sliced green onion

4 to 6 servings

In 2-quart casserole, combine water, grits and salt. Microwave at High for 3½ to 5 minutes, or until desired consistency. In 2-cup measure, blend half-and-half and eggs. Add egg mixture and remaining ingredients to grits. Mix well. Microwave at 70% (Medium High) for 10 to 14 minutes, or until heated through and mixture thickens, stirring twice.

To reheat: Place one serving on plate. Cover with wax paper. Microwave at 70% (Medium High) for 1½ to 2½ minutes, or until heated through, stirring once.

Cheese Grits
Fried Eggs   Melon & Strawberries   Apple Streusel Cake

Easy Beans & Rice

- ⅔ cup hot water
- ½ cup uncooked quick-cooking brown rice
- ½ cup chopped onion
- 1 clove garlic, minced
- 2 tablespoons butter or margarine
- ¼ teaspoon salt
- 1 can (16 oz.) Great Northern beans, drained
- 1 can (15 oz.) garbanzo beans, drained
- 1 can (8 oz.) whole tomatoes, drained and cut up
- ½ cup tomato juice
- 2 tablespoons molasses
- ½ teaspoon dry mustard
- ⅛ teaspoon pepper

4 to 6 servings

In 1½-quart casserole, combine water, rice, onion, garlic, butter and salt. Cover. Microwave at High for 5 minutes. Microwave at 50% (Medium) for 10 to 15 minutes, or until liquid is absorbed and rice is tender. Mix in remaining ingredients. Re-cover. Microwave at High for 10 to 15 minutes, or until flavors are blended, stirring once.

To reheat: Place one serving on plate. Cover with wax paper. Microwave at High for 2 to 3 minutes, or until heated through, stirring once.

Easy Beans & Rice
Sliced Apple, Banana & Melon Salad
Pickled Peppers
Granola Cookies

Red Beans with Rice ▲

- 1 cup chopped onion
- 1 clove garlic, minced
- 1 tablespoon vegetable oil
- 1 can (15½ oz.) kidney beans, drained
- 1 can (15½ oz.) kidney beans, undrained
- ¼ cup chili sauce
- ¼ teaspoon cayenne
- ¼ teaspoon dried thyme leaves
- ⅛ teaspoon pepper
- 1 bay leaf
- Hot cooked rice

4 to 6 servings

In 1½-quart casserole, combine onion, garlic and oil. Cover. Microwave at High for 3 to 4 minutes, or until onion is tender-crisp. Stir in kidney beans, chili sauce, cayenne, thyme, pepper and bay leaf. Microwave, uncovered, at High for 12 to 15 minutes, or until mixture thickens slightly and flavors are blended, stirring twice. Remove bay leaf. Serve over hot cooked rice.

To reheat: Place one serving on plate. Microwave at High for 1½ to 2½ minutes, or until heated through, stirring once.

Red Beans with Rice
Assorted Cheese Platter   Custard

Family Favorites/Meatless

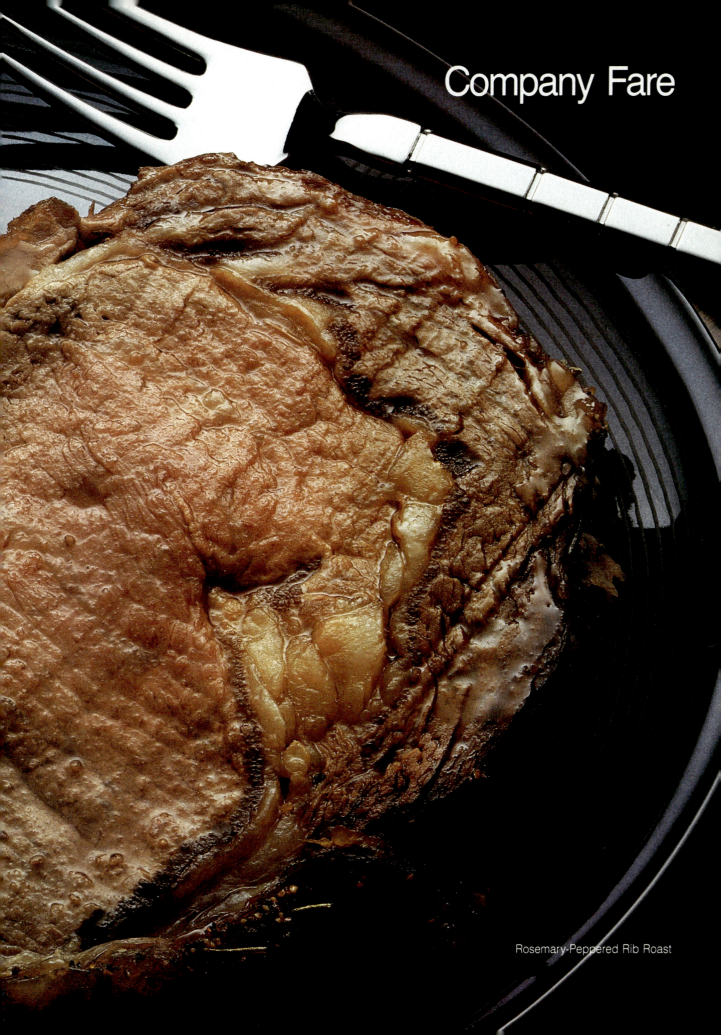

Company Fare

Rosemary-Peppered Rib Roast

Beef

◀ German Marinated Beef

- 2-lb. boneless beef top round steak, about 1 inch thick
- 3 tablespoons all-purpose flour
- 1 medium onion, thinly sliced
- ½ cup red wine vinegar
- ½ cup water
- 3 tablespoons honey
- 2 tablespoons vegetable oil
- 2 teaspoons whole mixed pickling spice
- ¾ teaspoon salt
- ¼ cup gingersnap cookie crumbs
- Dairy sour cream

6 to 8 servings

Pierce beef thoroughly with fork. Place flour in nylon cooking bag. Shake to coat. Add beef. Top with onion. Set aside. In 2-cup measure, mix wine vinegar, water, honey, oil, pickling spice and salt. Pour over steak and onion. Secure bag with nylon tie or string. Knead bag to mix in flour. Place bag on plate. Refrigerate for at least 24 hours, turning bag over once or twice.

Place beef in bag in 9-inch square baking dish in microwave oven. Microwave at High for 5 minutes. Microwave at 50% (Medium) for 40 to 50 minutes, or until beef is tender, turning beef over once. Let stand, covered, for 10 minutes. Remove beef to serving platter. Strain gravy. Pour 1 cup gravy over beef. Sprinkle beef with gingersnap crumbs. Top with sour cream. Serve remaining gravy with beef.

German Marinated Beef
Buttered New Potatoes & Sliced Celery
Baby Carrots   Pumpernickel Bread   Black Forest Cake

Rosemary-Peppered Rib Roast

- 3½ to 4-lb. boneless beef rolled rib roast
- 1 large clove garlic, cut into 6 slivers
- 2 teaspoons coarsely ground pepper
- ¾ teaspoon dried rosemary leaves

8 servings

Cut six 1-inch slits in beef roast. Insert garlic slivers in slits. In small bowl, combine pepper and rosemary. Rub or sprinkle mixture on all sides of roast. Place fat-side down on roasting rack. Estimate total cooking time at 12 to 15 minutes per pound. Microwave at High for 5 minutes. Microwave at 50% (Medium) for remaining part of first half of total cooking time. Turn roast fat-side up. Microwave at 50% (Medium) for second half of cooking time, or until internal temperature registers 125°F for medium-rare doneness. Let stand, tented loosely with foil, for 10 minutes before carving. Serve with tomato garnish (right) if desired.

Rosemary-Peppered Rib Roast
Twice-baked Potatoes   Peas & Pearl Onions
Strawberry Sorbet with Mint Leaves

How to Make a Tomato Garnish

Insert knife to center, starting one-third from top of small tomato. Alternate angles to obtain a saw-tooth cut. Remove and discard top one-third portion. Sprinkle freshly cut surface with grated Parmesan cheese and fresh snipped parsley.

Beef Tenderloin with Carrots & Leeks

- 2 slices bacon, cut into 1-inch pieces
- 3 tablespoons all-purpose flour
- 1 teaspoon instant beef bouillon granules
- ½ teaspoon bouquet garni seasoning
- ¾ cup water
- ½ cup white wine
- ½ teaspoon bouquet sauce
- 2 cups frozen baby carrots
- 1 cup thinly sliced leeks
- 1½ lbs. beef tenderloin, cut into ¾-inch pieces

4 to 6 servings

Place bacon in 2-quart casserole. Microwave at High for 2 to 3 minutes, or until brown and crisp, stirring once. Stir in flour, bouillon and bouquet garni seasoning. Blend in water, wine and bouquet sauce. Stir in carrots and leeks. Cover. Microwave at High for 14 to 18 minutes, or until mixture is thickened and carrots are tender, stirring twice. Stir in beef pieces. Re-cover. Microwave at High for 2 to 6 minutes, or until beef is desired doneness, stirring once.

Beef Tenderloin with Carrots & Leeks
Spinach & Cherry Tomato Salad   Popovers   Boston Cream Pie

Burgundy Beef with Peppers

- 1 pkg. (1.8 oz.) oxtail soup and recipe mix
- 1 cup water
- ½ cup burgundy wine
- ½ teaspoon dried marjoram leaves
- ⅛ teaspoon garlic powder
- ⅛ teaspoon pepper
- 2 lbs. boneless beef sirloin steak, about 1 inch thick, cut into ¼-inch strips
- 8 oz. fresh mushrooms, cut in half
- 1 medium green pepper, cut into ¼-inch strips

6 to 8 servings

Burgundy Beef with Peppers
White Rice
Watercress & Carrot Salad
Butter Brickle Ice Cream & Vanilla Wafers

How to Microwave Burgundy Beef with Peppers

Blend soup mix and water in 3-quart casserole. Cover. Microwave at High for 4 to 6 minutes, or until mixture is thickened, beating once with whisk.

Stir in wine, marjoram, garlic powder, pepper and beef strips. Re-cover. Microwave at 70% (Medium High) for 9 to 12 minutes, or until beef is tender and no longer pink, stirring once or twice.

Stir in mushrooms and green pepper. Re-cover. Microwave at 70% (Medium High) for 7 to 9 minutes, or until vegetables are tender, stirring once.

Pork

◀ Pork Chops with Whole Wheat-Prune Stuffing

- 4 pork loin chops, about 1¼ inches thick, with pocket for stuffing (8 to 9 oz. each)
- ¼ cup chopped celery
- 2 tablespoons sliced green onion
- 2 tablespoons butter or margarine
- ½ teaspoon dried marjoram leaves
- ½ teaspoon salt
- ½ teaspoon grated orange peel
- ⅛ teaspoon pepper
- 2 slices whole wheat bread, cut into ½-inch cubes
- ½ cup pitted prunes, cut up

4 servings

Brown chops conventionally on both sides. Set aside. In small mixing bowl, combine celery, onion and butter. Cover with plastic wrap. Microwave at High for 2 minutes. Stir in marjoram, salt, orange peel and pepper. Add bread cubes and prunes. Mix well. Fill each pocket with one-fourth of stuffing. Arrange chops on roasting rack with bone-side toward center of rack. Cover with wax paper. Microwave at 70% (Medium High) for 16 to 21 minutes, or until pork near bone is no longer pink, turning chops over and rotating rack once. Let stand, covered, for 3 minutes. Garnish each chop with orange zest (below) if desired.

Pork Chops with Whole Wheat-Prune Stuffing
Buttered Brussels Sprouts & Julienne Carrots
Spiced Apple Rings   Cherry Turnovers

How to Make an Orange Zest

Cut very thin strips of orange peel using a thin sharp knife or zester. Arrange thin strips on food as desired. Do not include white membrane of orange in strips.

Pork Medallions in Cream Sauce

- 1½ lbs. pork tenderloins, trimmed, sliced ½ inch thick
- ½ cup ready-to-serve chicken broth
- 2 tablespoons snipped fresh parsley
- 2 tablespoons sliced green onion
- 1 thin slice lemon
- ½ teaspoon salt
- ½ teaspoon dried thyme leaves
- Dash pepper
- ½ cup whipping cream
- 3 tablespoons all-purpose flour
- Lemon slices
- Fresh parsley

6 servings

Place pork in 1½-quart casserole. Stir in broth, parsley, onion, lemon, salt, thyme and pepper. Cover. Microwave at 70% (Medium High) for 14 to 17 minutes, or until pork is no longer pink, stirring 2 or 3 times. Remove pork with slotted spoon to serving platter. Cover. Set aside. Reserve cooking liquid in casserole. Place whipping cream in small mixing bowl. Stir in flour with whisk until smooth. Add cream mixture to cooking liquid. Blend well with whisk. Microwave, uncovered, at 50% (Medium) for 7 to 9 minutes, or until mixture thickens and bubbles, stirring twice with whisk. Pour sauce over pork. Garnish with lemon slices and fresh parsley.

Pork Medallions in Cream Sauce
Thin Egg Noodles
Sautéed Zucchini & Yellow Squash
Chocolate-dipped Strawberries

Braised Pork Chops with Sweet Peppers

- 1 medium onion, thinly sliced
- 1 clove garlic, minced
- 1 tablespoon olive oil
- 2 tablespoons all-purpose flour
- ½ teaspoon salt
- ⅛ teaspoon cayenne
- 4 butterflied pork chops, about ½ inch thick (6 to 8 oz. each)
- ⅓ cup ready-to-serve chicken broth
- 2 teaspoons lime juice
- 1 teaspoon Worcestershire sauce
- 1 medium red pepper, cut into ½-inch strips

4 servings

Braised Pork Chops with Sweet Peppers
Spinach & Fresh Mushroom Salad
Poppy Seed Rolls & Butter
Assorted Chocolate Truffles

How to Microwave Braised Pork Chops with Sweet Peppers

Combine onion, garlic and oil in 9-inch square baking dish. Cover with plastic wrap. Microwave at High for 3 to 4 minutes, or until onion is tender-crisp. In large plastic food storage bag, combine flour, salt and cayenne.

Add chops. Shake to coat. Arrange coated chops over onion and garlic. In 1-cup measure, combine broth, lime juice and Worcestershire sauce. Mix well.

Pour over chops. Cover with plastic wrap. Microwave at 70% (Medium High) for 10 minutes. Turn chops over. Stir sauce.

Fruited Pork Ragout

- 1 cup julienne rutabaga (2 × ½-inch strips)
- 1 medium onion, cut into 8 pieces
- 1 cup ready-to-serve chicken broth
- 1 can (17 oz.) apricot halves, drained (reserve ⅓ cup syrup)
- ¼ cup all-purpose flour
- ½ teaspoon fennel seed, crushed
- ½ teaspoon salt
- 1½ lbs. boneless pork loin, cut into 1-inch pieces
- ½ teaspoon bouquet sauce
- 1 medium cooking apple, cut into ½-inch cubes (about 1 cup)
- ½ cup raisins

6 servings

In 3-quart casserole, combine rutabaga, onion, broth and ⅓ cup apricot syrup. Cover. Microwave at High for 8 to 11 minutes, or until vegetables are tender-crisp, stirring twice. In large plastic food storage bag, combine flour, fennel and salt. Add pork pieces. Shake to coat. Add to vegetables. Stir in bouquet sauce, apple and raisins. Re-cover. Microwave at High for 5 minutes. Mix well. Microwave at 70% (Medium High) for 20 to 25 minutes, or until pork is tender and no longer pink, stirring twice. Stir in apricots. Let stand, covered, for 5 minutes.

Arrange red pepper strips on chops. Cover with plastic wrap. Microwave at 70% (Medium High) for 10 to 13 minutes, or until pork is no longer pink, rotating dish once. Let stand, covered, for 3 minutes.

Fruited Pork Ragout
Chilled Asparagus Spears on Lettuce Leaves
French Bread   Assorted Crisp Cookies

Lamb

◄ Summer Lamb Stew

- 2 tablespoons all-purpose flour
- 2 teaspoons sugar
- 1 clove garlic, minced
- ½ teaspoon dried marjoram leaves
- ½ teaspoon salt
- ⅛ teaspoon cayenne
- 2 lbs. boneless lamb shoulder, cut into ¾-inch pieces
- 1 can (28 oz.) whole tomatoes, cut up
- 4 cups trimmed fresh spinach leaves
- 1 cup sliced summer squash, ⅛ inch thick

4 to 6 servings

In 3-quart casserole, combine flour, sugar, garlic, marjoram, salt and cayenne. Mix well. Add lamb pieces. Toss to coat. Stir in tomatoes. Cover. Microwave at High for 5 minutes. Stir. Re-cover. Microwave at 50% (Medium) for 40 to 55 minutes, or until lamb is tender, stirring 2 or 3 times. Gently stir in spinach and summer squash. Re-cover. Microwave at High for 2 minutes. Let stand, covered, for 5 minutes.

Summer Lamb Stew
Couscous   Sesame Bread Sticks   Baklava

Lamb Chops with Minty Pear Sauce

- 4 lamb loin chops (4 to 5 oz. each)
- 1 can (16 oz.) pear halves, drained and cut into ½-inch strips (reserve syrup)
- 1 teaspoon packed brown sugar
- ½ teaspoon salt
- ½ teaspoon dried mint flakes
- ½ teaspoon grated orange peel
- 1 tablespoon cornstarch
- 1 tablespoon cold water

4 servings

Arrange chops in 9-inch square baking dish with bone-side toward center of dish. Set aside. Add water to pear syrup to equal ¾ cup. In small mixing bowl, combine pear syrup, brown sugar, salt, mint and orange peel. Mix well. Pour over chops. Cover with wax paper. Microwave at High for 5 minutes. Baste chops with cooking liquid. Re-cover. Microwave at 50% (Medium) for 10 to 13 minutes, or until lamb is medium doneness, basting once. Remove chops to serving plate. Cover. Set aside. In small bowl, blend cornstarch and water until smooth. Blend into cooking liquid. Microwave, uncovered, at High for 2 to 4 minutes, or until mixture is thickened and translucent, stirring once. Stir in pear slices. Microwave at High for 30 seconds to 1 minute, or until hot. Serve sauce over chops.

Lamb Chops with Minty Pear Sauce
Asparagus Spears with Pimiento
Caesar Salad
Napoleon Pastries

Veal

Walnut-Tarragon ▶ Veal Cutlets

- 1 egg, beaten
- 1 tablespoon lemon juice
- ⅔ cup unseasoned dry bread crumbs
- ¼ cup finely chopped walnuts
- 1 tablespoon dried parsley flakes
- ¾ teaspoon salt
- ½ teaspoon dried tarragon leaves
- ¼ teaspoon pepper
- ¾ lb. veal cutlets, about ¼ inch thick
- Lemon slices (optional)

4 servings

Walnut-Tarragon Veal Cutlets
Parsleyed New Potatoes
Broccoli & Sweet Red Peppers
Orange Sherbet & Wafer Cookies

How to Microwave Walnut-Tarragon Veal Cutlets

Line a 12-inch round platter with 2 layers of paper towels. Set aside. In 9-inch pie plate, blend egg and lemon juice. Set aside.

Mix bread crumbs, walnuts, parsley, salt, tarragon and pepper on sheet of wax paper. Dip veal in egg mixture, then in crumb mixture, pressing lightly to coat both sides.

Place cutlets on paper towel-lined platter. Microwave at 70% (Medium High) for 7 to 10 minutes, or until veal is firm rotating platter twice.

Saucy Veal & Mushrooms ▲

- 1 envelope (.87 oz.) white sauce mix
- 2 tablespoons snipped fresh parsley
- ½ teaspoon salt
- ⅛ teaspoon pepper
- ⅔ cup milk
- 8 oz. fresh mushrooms, thinly sliced
- 1½ lbs. veal round steak, about ½ inch thick, cut into ¼-inch strips
- ¼ cup dairy sour cream

6 to 8 servings

In 2-quart casserole, combine sauce mix, parsley, salt and pepper. Blend in milk. Beat well with whisk. Microwave at High for 3½ to 4½ minutes, or until mixture is very thick, stirring after every minute. Gently stir in mushrooms. Microwave at High for 2 minutes. Stir. Add veal strips. Stir. Cover. Microwave at 50% (Medium) for 15 to 20 minutes, or until veal is no longer pink, stirring once or twice. Stir in sour cream. Let stand, covered, for 5 to 10 minutes.

Saucy Veal & Mushrooms
Fettuccine   Romaine, Orange & Red Onion Salad
Herbed Peas & Carrots   Apple Pie with Spiced Whipped Cream

Cut lemon into thin slices. Cut each slice through the center, leaving one edge of peel intact. Twist slice into 'S' shape. Garnish veal with lemon twist.

Poultry

◄ Chicken in Spicy Peanut Sauce

- 1 cup coarsely chopped onion
- 1 clove garlic, minced
- 1 tablespoon vegetable oil
- 2½ to 3-lb. broiler-fryer chicken, cut into 8 pieces, skin removed
- 1 can (8 oz.) whole tomatoes, cut up
- ⅓ cup water
- ¼ cup chili sauce
- 1 teaspoon chili powder
- ½ teaspoon salt
- ¼ teaspoon ground ginger
- ¼ teaspoon dried crushed red pepper
- ½ cup chunky peanut butter
- Chopped tomato (optional)
- Sliced green onions (optional)
- Peanuts (optional)

4 servings

In 3-quart casserole, combine onion, garlic and oil. Cover. Microwave at High for 4 to 5 minutes, or until onion is tender, stirring once. Arrange chicken over onion.

In 2-cup measure, combine tomatoes, water, chili sauce, chili powder, salt, ginger and red pepper. Mix well. Pour over chicken. Re-cover. Microwave at High for 16 to 21 minutes, or until chicken near bone is no longer pink and juices run clear, rearranging chicken twice. Remove chicken to platter. Cover. Set aside.

Stir peanut butter into tomato mixture. Microwave at High for 2 minutes, stirring once. Serve sauce over chicken. Garnish with tomato, green onions and peanuts.

> **Chicken in Spicy Peanut Sauce**
> Curried Rice
> Papaya & Kiwi Fruit with Poppy Seed-Honey Dressing
> Flat Bread   Pineapple Sherbet

Chicken Breasts with Artichoke Sauce

- 2 tablespoons butter or margarine
- 1 tablespoon plus 1 teaspoon cornstarch
- ¼ teaspoon dried rosemary leaves, crushed
- ⅛ teaspoon salt
- 1 cup ready-to-serve chicken broth
- ¼ cup white wine
- 1 can (14 oz.) artichoke hearts, drained and quartered
- 2 bone-in whole chicken breasts (10 to 12 oz. each) split in half, skin removed

4 servings

Place butter in 4-cup measure. Microwave at High for 45 seconds to 1 minute, or until butter melts. Stir in cornstarch, rosemary and salt. Blend in broth and wine. Microwave at High for 4 to 8 minutes, or until sauce is thickened and translucent, stirring twice. Stir in artichoke pieces. Cover with plastic wrap. Set aside.

Arrange chicken in 9-inch square baking dish. Cover with wax paper. Microwave at High for 10 to 15 minutes, or until chicken near bone is no longer pink and juices run clear, rearranging chicken once or twice. If needed, microwave sauce at High for 30 seconds to 1 minute, or until hot, stirring once. Serve sauce over chicken.

> **Chicken Breasts with Artichoke Sauce**
> Herb-Rice Medley   Caesar Salad   Cherry Pie with Ice Cream

Chicken with Mornay Sauce

- 2 tablespoons butter or margarine
- 2 tablespoons all-purpose flour
- 1 teaspoon dried parsley flakes
- 1 teaspoon instant chicken bouillon granules
- Dash ground nutmeg
- 1 cup milk
- ½ cup shredded Swiss cheese
- 3 tablespoons white wine
- 2 bone-in whole chicken breasts (10 to 12 oz. each) split in half, skin removed
- 2 tablespoons sliced almonds

4 servings

Place butter in 4-cup measure. Microwave at High for 45 seconds to 1 minute, or until butter melts. Stir in flour, parsley, bouillon and nutmeg. Blend in milk. Microwave at High for 4 to 6½ minutes, or until mixture thickens and bubbles, stirring 2 or 3 times. Stir in cheese until melted. Blend in wine. Cover with plastic wrap. Set aside. Arrange chicken in 9-inch square baking dish. Cover with wax paper. Microwave at High for 10 to 15 minutes, or until chicken near bone is no longer pink and juices run clear, rearranging chicken once or twice. If needed, microwave sauce at High for 30 seconds to 1 minute, or until hot, stirring once. Serve sauce over chicken. Top with almonds. Garnish with orange zest (page 93) if desired.

Chicken with Mornay Sauce
Wild Rice with Celery
Asparagus
Fudge Nut Torte

Spicy Chicken Curry

- ½ cup chopped green pepper
- ¼ cup chopped onion
- 2 teaspoons curry powder
- ¼ teaspoon ground cinnamon
- 1 tablespoon olive oil
- 1 can (16 oz.) whole tomatoes, cut up
- 1 can (6 oz.) tomato paste
- ⅓ cup raisins
- 2 teaspoons packed brown sugar
- ¾ teaspoon salt
- 2 lbs. boneless whole chicken breasts, skin removed, cut into 1-inch strips
- 1 medium zucchini, diagonally sliced, ¼ inch thick

Spicy Oil:
- 2 tablespoons olive oil
- 1 teaspoon caraway seed, crushed
- ½ teaspoon cayenne

6 to 8 servings

Spicy Chicken Curry
White Rice
Boston & Iceberg Lettuce with Oil & Vinegar Dressing
Assorted Melon Slices, Grapes & Strawberries

How to Microwave Spicy Chicken Curry

Combine green pepper, onion, curry powder, cinnamon and olive oil in 2-quart casserole. Cover. Microwave at High for 3 to 5 minutes, or until green pepper is tender-crisp. Stir in tomatoes, tomato paste, raisins, brown sugar and salt. Re-cover.

Microwave at High for 8 to 10 minutes, or until flavors are blended, stirring once. Stir in chicken and zucchini. Re-cover. Microwave at High for 12 to 16 minutes, or until chicken is no longer pink, stirring twice. Let stand, covered, for 5 minutes.

Combine all Spicy Oil ingredients in small container. Cover. Shake to blend. Drizzle small amount over each serving.

Chinese Chicken with Vegetables

- 2 lbs. boneless whole chicken breasts, skin removed, cut into 1-inch pieces
- 2 tablespoons soy sauce
- 1 large green pepper, cut into 1-inch pieces
- 2 teaspoons cornstarch
- 1 teaspoon sugar
- ¼ teaspoon ground ginger
- ¼ teaspoon chili powder
- ⅛ teaspoon cayenne
- 1 tablespoon water
- 1 tablespoon Hoisin sauce
- 1 large tomato, cut into 12 wedges
- 1 jar (7 oz.) whole baby corn, drained

6 to 8 servings

Chinese Chicken with Vegetables
Soft Chinese Noodles
Egg Rolls
Lemon Sherbet with Fortune or Almond Cookies

How to Microwave Chinese Chicken with Vegetables

Combine chicken pieces and soy sauce in 2-quart casserole. Cover. Microwave at High for 6 to 9 minutes, or until chicken is no longer pink, stirring after every 2 minutes.

Remove chicken with slotted spoon to bowl. Cover. Set aside. Add green pepper to cooking liquid in casserole. Re-cover. Microwave at High for 3 to 4 minutes, or until green pepper is tender-crisp.

Add green pepper to chicken. Re-cover. Set aside. Reserve cooking liquid in casserole. In small bowl, combine cornstarch, sugar, ginger, chili powder, cayenne and water. Mix well.

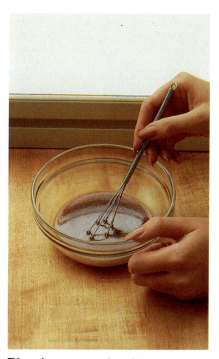

Blend cornstarch mixture and Hoisin Sauce into cooking liquid. Microwave, uncovered, at High for 2 to 4 minutes, or until mixture is thickened and translucent, stirring 2 or 3 times.

Stir in chicken, green pepper, tomato and corn. Toss gently to coat. Re-cover. Microwave at High for 3 to 5 minutes, or until hot, stirring once.

Basque-style Turkey Tenderloins ▲

- 1 tablespoon olive oil
- 1 teaspoon dried basil leaves
- 1 to 2 cloves garlic, minced
- 1 can (10½ oz.) condensed French onion soup
- ¼ cup white wine
- 2 lbs. turkey tenderloins, diagonally sliced ½ inch thick
- ½ cup pitted prunes
- ½ cup dried apricots

6 to 8 servings

In 10-inch square casserole, combine olive oil, basil and garlic. Cover. Microwave at High for 1 minute. Stir in soup and wine. Add turkey, prunes and apricots, stirring to coat. Re-cover. Microwave at 70% (Medium High) for 18 to 22 minutes, or until turkey is cooked through and no longer pink, stirring twice. Remove turkey and fruit with slotted spoon to platter.

Basque-style Turkey Tenderloins

*Broccoli Spears with Lemon Butter Sourdough Bread
Chocolate Mousse with Slivered Almonds*

Italian Turkey Cutlets

Sauce:
- 1 can (16 oz.) whole tomatoes, drained and chopped
- 3 tablespoons finely chopped onion
- 2 teaspoons olive oil
- ¾ teaspoon dried basil leaves
- ½ teaspoon dried parsley flakes
- ⅛ teaspoon dried crushed red pepper

- 1 egg, beaten
- 1 tablespoon milk
- 1 cup seasoned dry bread crumbs
- ⅛ teaspoon garlic powder
- ¾ to 1 lb. turkey cutlets, about ¼ inch thick
- 3 slices Provolone cheese, ⅛ inch thick, cut in half

4 to 6 servings

In small mixing bowl, combine all sauce ingredients. Mix well. Microwave at High for 5 to 9 minutes, or until onion is tender, stirring once. Set aside. In 9-inch pie plate, blend egg and milk. On sheet of wax paper, mix bread crumbs and garlic powder. Dip cutlets in egg mixture, then in crumb mixture, pressing lightly to coat both sides. Arrange on 12-inch round platter. Microwave, uncovered, at 70% (Medium High) for 5 to 8 minutes, or until turkey is firm, rearranging once. Do not turn cutlets over. Spoon sauce over turkey. Top with cheese. Microwave at 70% (Medium High) for 2 to 3 minutes, or until cheese melts, rotating platter once.

Italian Turkey Cutlets

*Antipasto Tray
Sautéed Zucchini
Italian Bread
Spumoni Ice Cream*

Turkey Cutlets with Gingered Peach Sauce

- 1 can (16 oz.) peach slices, drained
- ¼ cup golden raisins
- 1 teaspoon instant chicken bouillon granules
- ¼ teaspoon curry powder
- ¼ teaspoon ground ginger
- ¼ teaspoon salt
- ½ cup water
- 1 tablespoon cornstarch
- 1½ lbs. turkey cutlets, about ¼ inch thick
- Green onions (optional)

6 servings

In food processor or blender container, purée peach slices. In 4-cup measure, combine peach purée, raisins, bouillon, curry powder, ginger and salt. In 1-cup measure, blend water and cornstarch. Blend into peach mixture. Microwave at High for 5 to 6 minutes, or until mixture is thickened and translucent, stirring twice. Arrange cutlets in 10-inch square casserole. Cover with wax paper. Microwave at 70% (Medium High) for 11 to 17 minutes, or until turkey is firm and no longer pink, rearranging turkey once. Remove cutlets to serving platter. Spoon sauce over turkey. Microwave at 50% (Medium) for 6 to 8 minutes, or until sauce is heated through. Garnish with green onions.

Turkey Cutlets with Gingered Peach Sauce
Rice Pilaf   Green Beans Amandine   Endive & Watercress Salad   Chocolate Chip Pound Cake

Fish & Seafood

◄ Shellfish Dinner for Two

⅓ cup butter or margarine	2 tablespoons white wine
½ teaspoon bouquet garni seasoning	½ lb. mussels, scrubbed and beards removed
¼ teaspoon lemon pepper seasoning	½ lb. medium shrimp, shelled and deveined

2 servings

In 1-cup measure, combine butter, bouquet garni and lemon pepper. Microwave at High for 1½ to 1¾ minutes, or until butter melts. Blend in wine. Set aside. Arrange mussels on one side of 12-inch round platter. Arrange shrimp on other side of platter. Drizzle 2 tablespoons butter mixture evenly over shrimp. Cover with plastic wrap. Microwave at 50% (Medium) for 6 to 9 minutes, or until mussels open and shrimp are opaque, rotating platter once or twice. Let stand, covered, for 3 minutes. Arrange mussels and shrimp on serving platter. Serve with remaining butter mixture.

Shellfish Dinner for Two

Baked Potatoes with Sour Cream   Lettuce, Tomato & Cucumber Salad
Garlic Bread   Ice Cream with Hot Fudge Topping

Scallops with Coriander-Orange Sauce

1½ lbs. sea scallops	¼ teaspoon ground coriander
¼ cup sliced green onions	¼ teaspoon grated orange peel
¼ cup orange juice	2 tablespoons water
2 tablespoons white wine	2 tablespoons butter or margarine
1 tablespoon plus 1 teaspoon cornstarch	
¼ teaspoon salt	

6 servings

In 1½-quart casserole, combine scallops, onions, orange juice and wine. Cover. Microwave at 50% (Medium) for 10 to 13 minutes, or until scallops are firm and opaque, stirring twice. Remove scallops with slotted spoon to medium bowl. Cover. Set aside. Add water to cooking liquid to equal 1 cup. Return to casserole. Set aside. In small bowl, combine cornstarch, salt, coriander, orange peel and 2 tablespoons water. Mix well. Blend into cooking liquid. Add butter. Microwave at High for 3 to 4 minutes, or until mixture is thickened and translucent, stirring once or twice. Gently stir in scallops.

Scallops with Coriander-Orange Sauce

Wild Rice   French-style Green Beans with Almonds
French Bread   Chocolate Cream Pie

Company Fare/Fish & Seafood

Fish with Shrimp Sauce

- 1 lb. fish fillets, about ½ inch thick, cut into serving-size pieces
- 1 can (10¾ oz.) condensed cream of shrimp soup
- 2 tablespoons sherry
- 2 tablespoons snipped fresh parsley
- 2 teaspoons freeze-dried chives
- 1 teaspoon lemon juice
- ⅛ teaspoon pepper
- 1 can (4¼ oz.) large shrimp, rinsed and drained

6 servings

Arrange fish in 10-inch square casserole. Set aside. In small mixing bowl, combine soup, sherry, parsley, chives, lemon juice and pepper. Mix well. Gently stir in shrimp. Spoon shrimp sauce over fish. Cover with wax paper. Microwave at High for 7 to 11 minutes, or until fish flakes easily with fork, rearranging fish once. Let stand, covered, for 3 minutes.

Fish with Shrimp Sauce
Parsleyed White Rice
Peas & Mushrooms
Lemon Coconut Cake

Szechwan Shrimp ▲

- 1 tablespoon vegetable oil
- 1 clove garlic, minced
- ¼ teaspoon dried crushed red pepper
- ¼ teaspoon ground ginger
- ¼ cup oyster sauce
- 1 tablespoon chili sauce
- 1½ lbs. medium shrimp, shelled and deveined
- ¾ cup shredded carrots
- 1 jar (7 oz.) sliced shiitake mushrooms, drained
- ½ cup diagonally sliced green onions, ½ inch thick

6 servings

In 2-quart casserole, combine oil, garlic, red pepper and ginger. Cover. Microwave at High for 1 minute. Stir in oyster and chili sauces. Add shrimp, carrots, mushrooms and onions, stirring to coat. Cover with wax paper. Microwave at High for 7 to 10 minutes, or until shrimp are opaque, stirring 2 or 3 times. Let stand, covered, for 3 minutes.

Szechwan Shrimp
Soft Chinese Noodles
Fresh Bean Sprout & Pea Pod Salad with Toasted Sesame Seed Dressing
Vanilla Ice Cream with Fresh Pineapple Wedges

Salmon Steaks with Peppers

- ¼ cup butter or margarine
- 2 tablespoons lemon juice
- ¼ teaspoon onion salt
- ¼ teaspoon Italian seasoning
- 1 medium green pepper, cut into ¼-inch strips
- 1 medium yellow pepper, cut into ¼-inch strips
- 1 medium red pepper, cut into ¼-inch strips
- 4 salmon steaks (6 to 8 oz. each) about 1 inch thick

4 servings

Place butter in 10-inch square casserole. Microwave at High for 1¼ to 1½ minutes, or until butter melts. Stir in lemon juice, onion salt and Italian seasoning. Toss green, yellow and red pepper strips in butter mixture. Cover with wax paper. Microwave at High for 4 to 6 minutes, or until peppers are tender-crisp, stirring once. Arrange salmon steaks in casserole with thickest portions toward outside of casserole. Spoon peppers and cooking liquid over salmon. Re-cover. Microwave at 70% (Medium High) for 14 to 18 minutes, or until fish flakes easily with fork, rotating casserole and basting with cooking liquid once or twice.

Salmon Steaks with Peppers
Parsleyed Potato Slices   Bread Sticks
Raspberries with Grand Marnier & Custard Sauce

Company Fare/Fish & Seafood

Sole with Spicy Vegetable Sauce

- 1 can (16 oz.) whole tomatoes, drained and chopped
- 1 cup julienne zucchini (1½ × ¼-inch strips)
- ¼ cup sliced green onions
- ¼ cup chili sauce
- ¼ teaspoon salt
- ¼ teaspoon ground cumin
- ¼ teaspoon chili powder
- 6 sole fillets, about ¼ inch thick, 8 to 9 inches long
- 3 teaspoons dried parsley flakes
- 6 tablespoons shredded Monterey Jack cheese

6 servings

In 1-quart casserole, combine tomatoes, zucchini, onions, chili sauce, salt, cumin and chili powder. Mix well. Cover with wax paper. Microwave at High for 4 to 6 minutes, or until zucchini is tender, stirring once. Set aside. Sprinkle each fillet with ½ teaspoon parsley. Place 1 tablespoon cheese in center of each fillet. Roll up, enclosing filling. Place seam-side down in 9-inch square baking dish. Cover with wax paper. Microwave at High for 7 to 11 minutes, or until center of fish roll flakes easily with fork. Serve sauce over fish rolls.

Sole with Spicy Vegetable Sauce
Brown Rice   Avocado, Black Olive & Lettuce Salad
Pound Cake with Chocolate Ice Cream & Kahlua

◀ **Fillets with Buttery Filbert Sauce**

- ¼ cup plus 1 tablespoon butter or margarine, divided
- ⅓ cup coarsely chopped filberts
- 1½ lbs. orange roughy fillets, about ½ inch thick, cut into serving-size pieces
- ½ teaspoon dried tarragon leaves
- ¼ teaspoon salt
- 1 small orange, thinly sliced
- 2 tablespoons water
- 1 tablespoon cornstarch

6 servings

> **Fillets with Buttery Filbert Sauce**
> Buttered Broccoli Spears
> Romaine & Sliced Radish Salad
> Parkerhouse Rolls
> Frosted Spice Cake

How to Microwave Fillets with Buttery Filbert Sauce

Place 1 tablespoon butter in 9-inch pie plate. Microwave at High for 45 seconds to 1 minute, or until butter melts. Stir in filberts. Microwave at High for 3 to 4 minutes, or just until filberts are light golden brown, stirring after every minute.

Place filberts on 2 layers of paper towels. Set aside. Place remaining ¼ cup butter in 10-inch square casserole. Microwave at High for 1¼ to 1½ minutes, or until butter melts.

Dip fish in butter, turning to coat both sides. Arrange fish in casserole with thickest portions toward outside of casserole.

Sprinkle with tarragon and salt. Arrange orange slices over fish. Cover with wax paper. Microwave at High for 6 to 10 minutes, or until fish flakes easily with fork, rotating casserole once or twice.

Remove fish and orange slices to serving platter. Cover. Set aside. Add water to cooking liquid to equal ¾ cup.

Blend water and cornstarch in 2-cup measure until smooth. Blend cooking liquid into cornstarch mixture. Microwave at High for 1½ to 2½ minutes, or until mixture is thickened and translucent, stirring once or twice. Stir in toasted filberts. Serve sauce over fish.

Light & Easy

Warm Sirloin Salad

Beef

◄ Greek Kabobs

- 1 lb. boneless beef sirloin steak, about 1 inch thick, cut into 20 cubes
- 12 zucchini or yellow squash slices, ½ inch thick
- 4 pitted black olives
- 4 wooden skewers, 10-inch
- 2 tablespoons olive oil
- 1 tablespoon soy sauce
- 2 teaspoons lemon juice
- ½ teaspoon seasoned salt
- ⅛ teaspoon dried oregano leaves
- ⅛ teaspoon cayenne
- 4 cherry tomatoes

4 servings

For each kabob, alternate five beef cubes, three zucchini slices and a black olive on wooden skewer. Repeat to make 4 kabobs. Arrange on roasting rack. Set aside. In small bowl, combine olive oil, soy sauce, lemon juice, seasoned salt, oregano and cayenne. Mix well. Brush mixture on kabobs. Microwave at High for 6 to 8 minutes, or until beef is no longer pink, turning kabobs over, rearranging and brushing once with olive oil mixture. Add tomatoes during last minute of cooking.

> **Greek Kabobs**
> Rice Pilaf
> Red Grapes & Pear Slices

Italian Soup

- ½ lb. lean ground beef
- 4 cups hot water
- 1 pkg. (1.4 oz.) vegetable soup and recipe mix
- ½ cup uncooked elbow macaroni
- 1 can (8 oz.) tomato sauce
- 1 teaspoon sugar
- ¼ teaspoon Italian seasoning

4 servings

Crumble beef into 3-quart casserole. Cover. Microwave at High for 2 to 4 minutes, or until beef is no longer pink, stirring once to break apart. Stir in remaining ingredients. Re-cover. Microwave at High for 17 to 20 minutes, or until macaroni is tender, stirring twice.

To reheat: Place one serving in bowl. Cover with wax paper. Microwave at High for 2½ to 3½ minutes, or until heated through, stirring once.

> **Italian Soup**
> Seasoned Croutons   Grated Parmesan Cheese   Assorted Cookies

Warm Sirloin Salad

- 4 cups torn leaf lettuce
- 1 can (16 oz.) small whole beets, drained and sliced
- 1 large stalk celery, sliced
- ¼ cup vegetable oil
- 2 tablespoons red or white wine vinegar
- ½ teaspoon salt
- ½ teaspoon sugar
- ¼ teaspoon dried dill weed
- ⅛ teaspoon pepper
- ¾ to 1 lb. boneless beef sirloin steak, about 1 inch thick, cut into thin strips
- 1 small onion, thinly sliced, separated into rings

4 servings

Place lettuce on large serving platter. Arrange beets and celery over lettuce. Set aside. In 1-quart casserole, combine oil, vinegar, salt, sugar, dill weed and pepper. Mix well. Stir in beef strips and onion. Cover with wax paper. Microwave at 70% (Medium High) for 5 to 6½ minutes, or until beef is no longer pink, stirring twice. Remove beef and onion with slotted spoon to lettuce-lined platter. Spoon hot dressing over salad before serving.

> **Warm Sirloin Salad**
> Brick Cheese Slices   Rye Bread   Fruit Yogurt

Pepper & Mushroom Melt Burgers ▶

- 1 lb. lean ground beef
- 1 teaspoon Worcestershire sauce
- ½ teaspoon salt
- ⅛ teaspoon pepper
- ¼ teaspoon garlic powder, divided
- 1 can (4 oz.) sliced mushrooms, drained
- 2 tablespoons butter or margarine
- 4 slices (¾ oz. each) hot pepper cheese

4 servings

Pepper & Mushroom Melt Burgers
English Muffins
Lettuce Leaves & Tomato Slices
Carrot & Zucchini Sticks
Chocolate Chip Cookies

How to Microwave Pepper & Mushroom Melt Burgers

Combine beef, Worcestershire sauce, salt, pepper and ⅛ teaspoon garlic powder in medium mixing bowl. Mix well. Shape into four patties, about ½ inch thick. Arrange patties on roasting rack.

Quick Mexican Pizzas ▲

- 4 tostada shells
- ½ cup refried beans
- ½ lb. lean ground beef
- ¼ cup chopped onion
- 3 tablespoons hot salsa
- ⅛ teaspoon salt
- 1 cup shredded Monterey Jack cheese

2 to 4 servings

Line 12-inch round platter with paper towel. Arrange tostada shells on paper towel-lined platter. Spread 2 tablespoons refried beans over each tostada shell. Set aside. Crumble beef into 1-quart casserole. Add onion. Cover. Microwave at High for 3 to 4½ minutes, or until beef is no longer pink, stirring once to break apart. Drain. Stir in salsa and salt. Spoon one-fourth of beef mixture over each tostada shell. Top each with ¼ cup cheese. Microwave at 50% (Medium) for 3½ to 4½ minutes, or until cheese melts, rotating platter once.

Quick Mexican Pizzas
Lettuce, Tomato & Black Olive Salad   Sliced Kiwi Fruit & Blueberries

Microwave at High for 3 minutes. Turn patties over and rotate rack. Microwave at High for 2 to 4 minutes, or until patties are firm and no longer pink in center. Set aside.

Combine mushrooms, butter and remaining ⅛ teaspoon garlic powder in 1-quart casserole. Microwave at High for 1½ to 2½ minutes, or until butter melts, stirring once.

Top each patty with one-fourth of mushroom mixture and cheese slice. Microwave at High for 1½ to 2½ minutes, or until cheese melts, rotating rack once.

Light & Easy/Beef

Sprouts & Beef Pitas ▶

- 1 small red onion, sliced
- ¼ cup Italian dressing
- 4 frozen beef sandwich steaks (2 oz. each)
- 2 pita breads, 6-inch
- 2 slices (1 oz. each) Provolone cheese, cut in half
- 2 cups alfalfa sprouts

4 servings

Sprouts & Beef Pitas
Dill Pickle Spears
Assorted Chips
Oatmeal Raisin Cookies

How to Microwave Sprouts & Beef Pitas

Line 9-inch square baking dish with 2 layers of paper towels. Set aside. In 1-quart casserole, combine onion and Italian dressing. Cover. Microwave at High for 2 to 3 minutes, or until onion is tender-crisp, stirring once. Set aside.

Cut frozen steaks in half. Place four halves on roasting rack. Microwave at High for 3 to 4 minutes, or until beef is no longer pink, turning steaks over once. Repeat with remaining four steak halves.

Cut each pita bread in half. Fill each half with cheese, 2 steak halves, one-fourth of onions and one-fourth of alfalfa sprouts, reserving dressing from onions.

Chorizo Sausage Tacos

½ lb. chorizo sausages, diagonally sliced ¼ inch thick
⅓ cup mild taco sauce
2 tablespoons sliced green onion
6 taco shells

Toppings:
  Shredded lettuce
  Chopped tomatoes
  Chopped avocados
  Shredded Cheddar cheese
  Sliced black olives
  Dairy sour cream

6 servings

In 1-quart casserole, combine sausage, taco sauce and onion. Cover. Microwave at High for 4 to 6 minutes, or until sausage is thoroughly cooked, stirring once. Spoon mixture evenly into taco shells. Serve with desired toppings.

Chorizo Sausage Tacos
  Green Grapes   *Orange Sherbet*

Sprinkle 1 to 2 teaspoons reserved dressing over each pita filling. Place pita halves upright in paper towel-lined dish. Microwave at 70% (Medium High) for 2½ to 3½ minutes, or until sandwiches feel warm.

Pork

◀ **Bacon Spaghetti Sauce**

- ½ cup chopped onion
- 1 tablespoon olive oil
- 1 can (16 oz.) whole tomatoes, drained and cut up
- 1 can (15 oz.) tomato purée
- 1½ teaspoons sugar
- 1 teaspoon dried marjoram leaves
- ¼ teaspoon pepper
- 1 pkg. (6 oz.) Canadian bacon slices, cut into ½-inch strips

4 servings

In 1½-quart casserole, combine onion and olive oil. Microwave at High for 3 minutes. Stir in tomatoes, tomato purée, sugar, marjoram and pepper. Cover with wax paper. Microwave at High for 13 to 16 minutes, or until flavors are blended, stirring twice. Stir in Canadian bacon. Re-cover. Microwave at High for 3 to 4 minutes, or until heated through.

To reheat: Place one serving in bowl. Cover with wax paper. Microwave at High for 2 to 3 minutes, or until heated through, stirring once.

Bacon Spaghetti Sauce
Spaghetti
Grated Parmesan Cheese
Marinated Vegetables
Chocolate Wafer Cookies

Ham & Corn Chowder

- ¼ cup chopped green pepper
- 1 tablespoon butter or margarine
- 2 cups milk
- 1 cup water
- 1 cup frozen whole kernel corn
- 1 to 1½ cups cubed fully cooked ham, ½-inch cubes
- 1 cup instant mashed potato flakes
- 1 teaspoon instant chicken bouillon granules
- 1 teaspoon dried parsley flakes
- 1 teaspoon instant minced onion

4 servings

In 2-quart casserole, combine green pepper and butter. Cover. Microwave at High for 2 minutes. Add remaining ingredients. Mix well. Re-cover. Microwave at High for 14 to 18 minutes, or until mixture thickens, stirring twice.

To reheat: Place one serving in bowl. Cover with wax paper. Microwave at High for 2½ to 3½ minutes, or until heated through, stirring once.

Ham & Corn Chowder
Lettuce & Sliced Carrot Salad   Whole Wheat Rolls   Banana Cake

Hot Tortellini Salad

- 1 pkg. (8 oz.) cheese-filled tortellini
- ¼ cup butter or margarine
- 2 cups fresh broccoli flowerets
- ¼ cup sliced green onions
- 6 oz. fully cooked ham slices, about ⅛ inch thick, cut into ½-inch strips
- ½ cup dairy sour cream
- ½ teaspoon dried basil leaves
- ¼ teaspoon salt

4 to 6 servings

Hot Tortellini Salad
Bread Sticks
Raspberries & Cantaloupe

How to Microwave Hot Tortellini Salad

Prepare tortellini as directed on package. Rinse and drain. Set aside. Place butter in 2-quart casserole. Microwave at High for 1¼ to 1½ minutes, or until butter melts.

Stir in broccoli and onions. Cover. Microwave at High for 3 to 4 minutes, or until broccoli is tender-crisp, stirring once.

Stir in tortellini and remaining ingredients. Re-cover. Microwave at High for 3 to 4 minutes, or until hot, stirring once.

Poultry

◄ Chicken & Linguine

- 1 pkg. (7 oz.) linguine
- 2 tablespoons olive oil
- 1½ lbs. boneless whole chicken breasts, skin removed, cut into ½-inch strips
- 1 tablespoon lemon juice
- ¼ teaspoon dried oregano leaves
- 1 jar (6 oz.) marinated artichoke hearts, drained (reserve marinade)
- 1 cup julienne carrots (2 × ¼-inch strips)
- 1 medium green pepper, cut into thin strips
- 1 teaspoon sugar
- 8 oz. fresh mushrooms, sliced

6 servings

Prepare linguine as directed on package. Rinse and drain. Toss with olive oil. Cover. Set aside. In 2-quart casserole, combine chicken, lemon juice and oregano. Cover. Microwave at High for 5 to 7 minutes, or until chicken is no longer pink, stirring twice. Remove chicken with slotted spoon to platter. Cover. Set aside. Reserve 2 tablespoons cooking liquid in casserole. Add reserved artichoke marinade, carrots, green pepper and sugar to cooking liquid. Toss to coat. Cover. Microwave at High for 4 to 6 minutes, or until carrots are tender-crisp, stirring once. Stir in artichoke hearts and mushrooms. Re-cover. Microwave at High for 1½ to 2 minutes, or just until mushrooms are tender. Arrange linguine on platter. Top with chicken and vegetables. Drizzle with warm cooking liquid.

Chicken & Linguine
Sliced Peaches   Crisp Bread Sticks   Lemon Sherbet

Hot Smoked Turkey Salad

- 1 pkg. (7 oz.) macaroni rings
- ½ cup mayonnaise
- ¼ cup dairy sour cream
- 2 tablespoons sliced green onion
- 2 teaspoons honey
- 1 teaspoon poppy seed
- 1 teaspoon prepared mustard
- ½ lb. smoked cooked turkey breast, cut into thin strips
- 1 can (11 oz.) mandarin oranges, drained
- 1 cup seedless green grapes

4 servings

Prepare macaroni as directed on package. Rinse and drain. Set aside. In 2-quart casserole, combine mayonnaise, sour cream, onion, honey, poppy seed and mustard. Mix well. Stir in macaroni and turkey. Microwave at High for 3 to 6 minutes, or until heated through, stirring once. Gently stir in mandarin oranges and grapes.

Hot Smoked Turkey Salad
Celery & Carrot Sticks, Radishes & Olives
Crescent Dinner Rolls
Oatmeal Cookies

Barbecued Chicken Sandwich

- 1 pkg. (12 oz.) frozen breaded chicken patties
- ¼ cup barbecue sauce
- 4 slices Colby cheese, ⅛ inch thick

4 servings

Place 2 paper towels on plate. Arrange chicken patties on paper towel-lined plate. Microwave at High for 3 minutes. Turn patties over and rotate plate. Microwave at High for 1 to 3 minutes, or until chicken is heated through. Spread 1 tablespoon barbecue sauce on each patty. Top each with cheese slice. Microwave at High for 1½ to 2 minutes, or until cheese melts, rotating plate once.

Barbecued Chicken Sandwich
Poppy Seed Buns
Cole Slaw
Apple Wedges

Chicken & Vegetables with Bulgur ▲

- 1½ cups hot water
- 1 teaspoon instant chicken bouillon granules
- ¼ teaspoon onion powder
- ⅛ teaspoon salt
- ½ cup bulgur or cracked wheat
- 1½ lbs. boneless whole chicken breasts, skin removed, cut into 1½-inch pieces
- 1 medium tomato, seeded and coarsely chopped
- 1 cup quartered fresh mushrooms
- ½ cup chopped green pepper
- ¼ to ½ cup herb and spice dressing
- Dash pepper

4 to 6 servings

In small mixing bowl, combine water, bouillon, onion powder and salt. Mix well. Microwave at High for 3 to 6 minutes, or until water boils. Stir in bulgur. Cover with plastic wrap. Let stand about 30 minutes, or until bulgur softens. Drain and press to remove excess moisture. Spread bulgur on large serving platter.

Meanwhile, in 2-quart casserole, combine chicken, tomato, mushrooms and green pepper. Cover. Microwave at High for 7 to 10 minutes, or until chicken is no longer pink, stirring twice. Remove chicken and vegetables with slotted spoon. Place over bulgur. In 1-cup measure, combine dressing and pepper. Pour evenly over chicken and vegetables. Serve warm.

Chicken & Vegetables with Bulgur
Apple or Pear Slices   Zucchini Nut Bread

Cheesy Chicken Potato Topper

- 4 medium baking potatoes (8 oz. each)
- 3 tablespoons butter or margarine
- 3 tablespoons all-purpose flour
- ½ teaspoon instant minced onion
- ¼ teaspoon salt
- ⅛ teaspoon pepper
- ⅛ teaspoon dried thyme leaves
- 1¼ cups milk
- 1 can (6¾ oz.) chunk chicken
- ½ cup frozen peas and carrots
- ½ cup shredded Monterey Jack or Swiss cheese

4 servings

Cheesy Chicken Potato Topper
Tomato & Cucumber Salad
Whole Grain Dinner Rolls
Strawberry Sorbet

How to Microwave Cheesy Chicken Potato Topper

Pierce potatoes with fork. Arrange in circular pattern on paper towel in microwave oven. Microwave at High for 10 to 14 minutes, or until tender, turning potatoes over and rearranging after half the time. Wrap each potato in foil. Set aside.

Place butter in 1-quart casserole. Microwave at High for 1 to 1¼ minutes, or until butter melts. Stir in flour, onion, salt, pepper and thyme. Blend in milk. Microwave at High for 4 to 6 minutes, or until mixture thickens and bubbles, stirring after every minute.

Stir in chicken and peas and carrots. Microwave at High for 3 to 4½ minutes, or until vegetables are tender and mixture is heated through, stirring once. Stir in cheese until melted. Cut each potato in half lengthwise. Serve chicken mixture over potatoes.

How to Microwave Broccoli-topped Turkey Patties

Broccoli-topped Turkey Patties

- 4 slices bacon
- 1 pkg. (10 oz.) frozen broccoli in cheese sauce
- 1 lb. ground turkey
- 1 egg, slightly beaten
- 2 tablespoons unseasoned dry bread crumbs
- 2 teaspoons Dijon mustard
- ¼ teaspoon salt
- ⅛ teaspoon pepper

4 servings

Broccoli-topped Turkey Patties
Toasted English Muffins
Cucumber Slices
Frozen Fudge Bars

Place bacon on roasting rack. Cover with paper towel. Microwave at High for 3 to 5 minutes, or until brown and crisp. Cool slightly. Crumble. Set aside.

Slit broccoli pouch and place in shallow bowl. Microwave at High for 6 to 8 minutes, or until broccoli is tender, flexing pouch once. Cover. Set aside.

Combine turkey, egg, bread crumbs, mustard, salt and pepper in medium mixing bowl. Mix well.

Shape into 4 patties, about ½ inch thick. Arrange patties on roasting rack. Microwave at High for 4 minutes. Turn patties over and rotate rack.

Microwave at High for 3 to 6 minutes, or until firm and cooked through. If needed, microwave broccoli mixture at High for 1 minute, or until hot. Top each patty with broccoli mixture. Sprinkle with bacon.

Chicken & Pea Pod Medley

- 1 pkg. (6 oz.) frozen pea pods
- 1 pkg. (6 oz.) frozen rice medley
- 1½ cups cut-up cooked chicken or turkey
- 2 tablespoons butter or margarine
- ⅛ teaspoon ground ginger
- ⅛ teaspoon pepper
- 1 tablespoon soy sauce

2 to 4 servings

Unwrap pea pods and place on plate. Microwave at High for 2 to 2½ minutes, or until defrosted. Drain. Set aside. Unwrap frozen rice and place in 1½-quart casserole. Cover. Microwave at High for 3 to 4 minutes, or until hot, stirring once to break apart. Stir in chicken and pea pods. Re-cover. Microwave at High for 2 to 4 minutes, or until heated through, stirring once. Set aside. In 1-cup measure, combine butter, ginger and pepper. Microwave at High for 45 seconds to 1 minute, or until butter melts. Stir in soy sauce. Pour over chicken mixture. Toss to coat.

Chicken & Pea Pod Medley
Fresh Pineapple Wedges   Fortune Cookies

Turkey & Leek Soup ▶

- ½ cup chopped carrot
- 1 tablespoon butter or margarine
- 1 pkg. (2.4 oz.) leek soup and recipe mix
- ⅛ teaspoon pepper
- 2⅓ cups hot water
- ½ cup milk
- 1½ cups cut-up cooked turkey or chicken
- ⅓ cup uncooked instant rice

4 servings

In 3-quart casserole, combine carrot and butter. Cover. Microwave at High for 2 to 4 minutes, or until carrot is tender-crisp, stirring once. Stir in soup mix and pepper. Blend in water and milk. Stir in turkey. Re-cover. Microwave at High for 10 to 14 minutes, or until mixture is slightly thickened, stirring twice. Stir in rice. Let stand, covered, for 5 minutes.

To reheat: Place one serving in bowl. Cover with wax paper. Microwave at High for 2 to 3 minutes, or until heated through, stirring once.

Turkey & Leek Soup
Cheese & Crackers
Angel Food Cake with Sliced Strawberries

Creamy Turkey & Vegetables

- 1½ cups hot water
- 1 pkg. (5 oz.) noodles and primavera sauce mix
- ½ cup milk
- 2 cups frozen broccoli, cauliflower and carrot medley
- 1½ cups cut-up cooked turkey or chicken
- ⅛ teaspoon pepper
- 2 tablespoons dairy sour cream

4 servings

Place water in 2-quart casserole. Cover. Microwave at High for 3 to 6 minutes, or until water boils. Stir in noodles and sauce mix, milk, vegetables, turkey and pepper. Microwave, uncovered, at High for 10 to 14 minutes, or until noodles are tender and sauce thickens, stirring twice. Stir in sour cream. Let stand, covered, for 10 minutes.

To reheat: Place one serving in bowl. Cover with wax paper. Microwave at 70% (Medium High) for 2 to 3 minutes, or until heated through, stirring once.

Creamy Turkey & Vegetables
Cranberry Relish   Lemon Bars

Fish & Seafood

Grouper with Dijon Butter

1 lb. grouper fillets, about 1 inch thick, cut into serving-size pieces	2 teaspoons honey
	2 teaspoons lemon juice
	¼ teaspoon salt
¼ cup butter or margarine	⅛ teaspoon dried thyme leaves
1 tablespoon Dijon mustard	

4 servings

Arrange grouper in 9-inch square baking dish with thickest portions toward outside of dish. Set aside. Place butter in 1-cup measure. Microwave at High for 1¼ to 1½ minutes, or until butter melts. Stir in mustard, honey, lemon juice, salt and thyme. Mix well. Pour over grouper. Cover with wax paper. Microwave at High for 8 to 12 minutes, or until fish flakes easily with fork, spooning sauce over fish and rotating dish twice.

To reheat: Place one serving on plate. Cover with wax paper. Microwave at 70% (Medium High) for 2½ to 3½ minutes, or until heated through.

Grouper with Dijon Butter
Spinach Egg Noodles   Romaine & Mandarin Orange Salad
Sugar Cookies

◀ Shrimp & Broccoli Teriyaki

1 pkg. (12 oz.) frozen uncooked large shrimp	1 tablespoon honey
	1 tablespoon vegetable oil
3 cups fresh broccoli flowerets	1½ cups thinly sliced fresh mushrooms
¼ cup sliced green onions	
¼ cup teriyaki sauce	Spinach leaves

4 servings

Place shrimp in 2-quart casserole. Cover. Microwave at 70% (Medium High) for 8 to 13 minutes, or until shrimp are opaque, stirring after every 2 minutes. Drain. Set aside. In same casserole, combine broccoli and onions. Set aside. In small bowl, combine teriyaki sauce, honey and oil. Pour over broccoli and onions. Cover. Microwave at High for 4 to 5 minutes, or until broccoli is tender-crisp, stirring once. Stir in mushrooms. Re-cover. Microwave at High for 1 minute. Gently stir in shrimp. Serve on spinach leaves.

Shrimp & Broccoli Teriyaki
Fried Rice   Orange Sherbet

Hot Rotini & Seafood Salad

- 2 cups uncooked rotini pasta
- 1 pkg. (10 oz.) frozen asparagus cuts
- ¾ lb. medium shrimp, shelled and deveined
- 8 seafood sticks (1 oz. each) cut into 1-inch pieces
- 3 tablespoons butter or margarine
- 2 teaspoons lemon juice
- ½ teaspoon dried dill weed
- ⅛ teaspoon garlic powder
- ⅛ teaspoon pepper

6 to 8 servings

Prepare rotini as directed on package. Rinse and drain. Set aside. Unwrap asparagus and place on plate. Microwave at High for 3 to 4 minutes, or until defrosted. Drain.

In 3-quart casserole, combine rotini, asparagus, shrimp and seafood pieces. Mix well. Cover. Microwave at High for 6 to 10 minutes, or until shrimp are opaque, stirring 2 or 3 times.

In 1-cup measure, combine remaining ingredients. Microwave at High for 1¼ to 1½ minutes, or until mixture is hot and bubbly. Stir. Pour over seafood mixture. Toss to coat. Serve with lemon wedges, if desired.

Hot Rotini & Seafood Salad
Orange Sections
Granola Cookies

Trout & Mushroom Sauce

- 8 oz. fresh mushrooms, coarsely chopped
- ¼ cup chopped onion
- 2 tablespoons butter or margarine
- 1 can (16 oz.) whole tomatoes, cut up
- 1 can (6 oz.) tomato paste
- 1 to 1½ teaspoons Italian seasoning
- 1 teaspoon dried parsley flakes
- 1 teaspoon sugar
- ¼ teaspoon pepper
- ¾ to 1 lb. trout fillets, about ½ inch thick, cut into 1½-inch pieces

4 to 6 servings

In 2-quart casserole, combine mushrooms, onion and butter. Cover. Microwave at High for 4 to 6 minutes, or until mushrooms are tender, stirring once.

Stir in remaining ingredients, except fish. Re-cover. Microwave at High for 15 to 20 minutes, or until flavors are blended, stirring twice. Stir in fish. Re-cover. Microwave at High for 5 to 8 minutes, or until fish flakes easily with fork, stirring once.

To reheat: Place one serving in bowl. Cover with wax paper. Microwave at High for 2 to 3½ minutes, or until heated through, stirring once.

Trout & Mushroom Sauce
Rigatoni
Chilled Asparagus Spears with Oil & Vinegar Dressing
Wafer Cookies

Summer Tuna Platter ▲

- 1 lb. small red potatoes, 2 inches each
- 1 can (16½ oz.) three bean salad, drained (reserve ¼ cup liquid)
- ¼ teaspoon dried basil leaves
- 1 tablespoon olive oil
- 1 teaspoon lemon juice
- Dash pepper
- Leaf lettuce
- 1 can (12½ oz.) water pack tuna, drained and flaked
- ¼ cup sliced black olives

6 servings

Remove ½-inch strip around center of each potato. Place potatoes in 1½-quart casserole. Add reserved bean salad liquid. Sprinkle potatoes with basil. Cover.

Microwave at High for 7 to 10 minutes, or until potatoes are tender, stirring twice. Remove potatoes with slotted spoon. Set aside. Blend olive oil, lemon juice and pepper into cooking liquid in casserole. Set aside.

Arrange lettuce on large platter. Arrange potatoes and three bean salad around outer edge of platter. Arrange tuna in center of lettuce-lined platter. Top with olives. Drizzle dressing over salad.

Summer Tuna Platter
Bran Muffins   Frozen Fruit Juice Bars

Crab & Spinach-stuffed Shells ▶

- 12 uncooked jumbo pasta shells
- 1 pkg. (10 oz.) frozen spinach in butter sauce
- 1 pkg. (3 oz.) cream cheese
- 1 can (6 oz.) crab meat, rinsed, drained and cartilage removed
- ¼ cup shredded carrot
- ½ teaspoon dried basil leaves, divided
- ½ teaspoon salt, divided
- 2 tablespoons butter or margarine
- 2 tablespoons all-purpose flour
- 1 cup milk
- 1 tablespoon grated Parmesan cheese

4 to 6 servings

Crab & Spinach-stuffed Shells
Sliced Tomatoes
Garlic Toast
Chocolate Mint Cookies

How to Microwave Crab & Spinach-stuffed Shells

Prepare shells as directed on package. Rinse and drain. Set aside. Slit spinach pouch and place on plate. Microwave at High for 6 to 8 minutes, or until hot, flexing pouch once.

Place cream cheese in medium mixing bowl. Microwave at High for 15 to 30 seconds, or until softened. Add spinach, crab, carrot, ¼ teaspoon basil and ¼ teaspoon salt. Mix well. Spoon mixture into shells.

Place shells in 10-inch square casserole. Set aside. Place butter in 2-cup measure. Microwave at High for 45 seconds to 1 minute, or until butter melts.

Light & Easy/Fish & Seafood

Crab Soup

- 1 cup cubed red potatoes, ½-inch cubes
- ⅓ cup chopped onion
- 1 tablespoon vegetable oil
- 3 cups hot water
- 1 can (8 oz.) whole tomatoes, drained and cut up
- 2 teaspoons instant chicken bouillon granules
- ¼ teaspoon ground turmeric
- ⅛ teaspoon dried thyme leaves
  Dash pepper
- 1 can (6 oz.) crab meat, rinsed, drained and cartilage removed, or 1½ cups crab meat
- ½ cup frozen peas

4 servings

In 2-quart casserole, combine potatoes, onion and oil. Cover. Microwave at High for 3 to 4 minutes, or until onion is tender-crisp, stirring once. Stir in water, tomatoes, bouillon, turmeric, thyme and pepper. Re-cover. Microwave at High for 14 to 17 minutes, or until potatoes are tender, stirring 2 or 3 times. Stir in crab and peas. Re-cover. Microwave at High for 3 to 4 minutes, or until peas are tender, stirring once.

To reheat: Place one serving in bowl. Cover with wax paper. Microwave at High for 2½ to 3½ minutes, or until heated through, stirring once.

> *Crab Soup*
> *Cheese Croissants*
> *Melon Wedges*

Stir in flour, remaining ¼ teaspoon basil and remaining ¼ teaspoon salt. Blend in milk. Microwave at High for 4 to 6 minutes, or until mixture thickens and bubbles, stirring twice.

Pour evenly over stuffed shells. Cover with wax paper. Microwave at 70% (Medium High) for 4 to 5 minutes, or until heated through. Sprinkle with cheese.

Light & Easy/Fish & Seafood 137

Salmon-Rice Salad

1 pkg. (4.4 oz.) long grain and wild rice mix
2 cups water
1 tablespoon butter or margarine
1 tablespoon lemon juice
⅛ teaspoon dried thyme leaves
1 cup thinly sliced celery
1 can (11 oz.) mandarin oranges
1 can (6¾ oz.) skinless, boneless salmon, drained

4 servings

In 2-quart casserole, combine rice mix, water, butter, lemon juice and thyme. Cover. Microwave at High for 12 to 15 minutes, or until liquid is absorbed and rice is tender, stirring twice. Stir in celery. Re-cover. Microwave at High for 2 to 3 minutes, or until celery is tender-crisp. Cool slightly. Gently stir in mandarin oranges and salmon. Serve warm.

Salmon-Rice Salad
Buttered Pea Pods   Soft Bread Sticks   Fruit Yogurt

How to Microwave Smoked Salmon Omelet

Smoked Salmon Omelet

- 2 tablespoons butter or margarine, divided
- ½ cup chopped red pepper
- ¼ cup sliced green onions
- 3 oz. smoked salmon, flaked (about ½ cup)
- 4 eggs, separated
- 2 tablespoons milk
- ¼ teaspoon baking powder
- ¼ cup shredded Cheddar cheese

4 servings

Smoked Salmon Omelet
Spinach & Cherry Tomato Salad
Blueberry Muffins

Combine 1 tablespoon butter, the red pepper and onions in small mixing bowl. Cover with plastic wrap. Microwave at High for 2 to 4 minutes, or until pepper is tender-crisp, stirring once. Stir in salmon. Set aside.

Beat egg whites at high speed of electric mixer in large mixing bowl until stiff but not dry. Set aside. In small mixing bowl, combine egg yolks, milk and baking powder. Beat until thick and lemon-colored.

Gently fold egg yolk mixture into egg whites, using a rubber spatula. Place remaining 1 tablespoon butter in 9-inch pie plate. Microwave at High for 45 seconds to 1 minute, or until butter melts. Tilt plate to coat bottom and sides. Pour egg mixture into pie plate.

Place plate on saucer in microwave oven. Microwave at 50% (Medium) for 6 to 10 minutes, or until set, lifting edges of omelet with spatula after every 2 minutes so uncooked portion spreads evenly.

Spoon salmon mixture over half of omelet. Loosen omelet with spatula and fold in half. Sprinkle with cheese. Microwave at 50% (Medium) for 1½ to 3 minutes, or until cheese melts.

Light & Easy/Fish & Seafood

Cheese-filled Manicotti

Make-Ahead

Just before dinner may not always be the best time to cook. Take a free evening or week-end afternoon, cook at leisure, and be ready for the days when you're too busy to prepare dinner from scratch. This section offers several imaginative approaches to make-ahead cooking.

Get a head start on dinner with freezer meatballs, meat sauce or vegetable sauce. With these basic starters in the freezer, the time-consuming work is done in advance. All you do at dinner time is assemble the dish and give it a final microwaving. For variety, recipes for three totally different dinners accompany each basic recipe, which makes two to three meals.

Batch cooking solves your problem in a different way. Each recipe makes 8 servings and provides directions for heating one serving or four at a time. These fully cooked main dishes go from freezer to microwave to table. For true flexibility, try the make-ahead cabbage rolls or stuffed manicotti.

Make-Ahead 141

Meatballs & Mostaccioli

Meatball Soup

Meatball & Potato Dinner

Meatballs & Mostaccioli

- 2 cups uncooked mostaccioli
- ½ cup coarsely chopped green pepper
- 1 jar (15 oz.) spaghetti sauce
- 1 pkg. frozen Make-Ahead Freezer Meatballs, right
- 1 cup shredded Cheddar cheese

4 servings

Prepare mostaccioli as directed on package. Rinse and drain. Set aside. Place green pepper in 2-quart casserole. Cover. Microwave at High for 1 to 2 minutes, or until green pepper is tender-crisp. Stir in spaghetti sauce and frozen meatballs. Re-cover. Microwave at High for 7 to 10 minutes, or until meatballs are defrosted, stirring once. Stir in mostaccioli. Re-cover. Microwave at High for 7 to 12 minutes, or until meatballs are heated through, stirring once. Sprinkle with cheese. Re-cover. Microwave at High for 1 to 1½ minutes, or until cheese melts.

Meatballs & Mostaccioli
Spinach & Orange Salad   Hard Rolls   Vanilla Ice Cream with Hot Fudge

Meatball Soup

- 4½ cups water
- 1 can (16 oz.) whole tomatoes, cut up
- 1 cup frozen whole kernel corn
- ½ cup uncooked alphabet macaroni
- 1 tablespoon plus 1 teaspoon instant beef bouillon granules
- 2 teaspoons instant minced onion
- ¼ teaspoon pepper
- 1 pkg. frozen Make-Ahead Freezer Meatballs, right

6 to 8 servings

In 3-quart casserole, combine all ingredients, except meatballs. Mix well. Stir in frozen meatballs. Cover with wax paper. Microwave at High for 28 to 38 minutes, or until macaroni is tender, stirring 3 times.

Meatball Soup
Cheese & Crackers
Carrot & Celery Sticks
Brownies

Meatball & Potato Dinner

- 1 pkg. (5.25 oz.) sour cream and chive potatoes mix (reserve seasoning packet)
- 2½ cups hot water
- 2 tablespoons butter or margarine
- ½ cup milk
- 1 pkg. frozen Make-Ahead Freezer Meatballs, right
- 1 cup frozen cut green beans

4 to 6 servings

In 3-quart casserole, combine potatoes, water and butter. Cover. Microwave at High for 10 minutes. Add contents of seasoning packet and milk. Mix well. Stir in frozen meatballs and green beans. Re-cover. Microwave at High for 16 to 23 minutes, or until potatoes are tender and sauce thickens, stirring 2 or 3 times. Let stand, covered, for 5 minutes.

Meatball & Potato Dinner
Spinach & Mushroom Salad
Dinner Rolls
Orange Cake

Make-Ahead Freezer Meatballs

- 3 lbs. ground beef
- 1½ cups soft bread crumbs
- 2 eggs, slightly beaten
- ⅓ cup finely chopped onion
- ¼ cup milk
- 1 tablespoon dried parsley flakes
- 2 teaspoons salt
- ½ teaspoon dried thyme leaves
- ½ teaspoon pepper
- ¼ teaspoon garlic powder

3 containers
18 meatballs each

Combine all ingredients in large mixing bowl. Mix well. Shape into 54 meatballs, about 1½ inches each. Place 18 meatballs in 2-quart casserole. Cover with wax paper. Microwave at High for 4½ to 6½ minutes, or just until meatballs are firm and no longer pink, gently rearranging twice. Drain. Remove to wax paper-lined tray. Repeat with remaining meatballs. Freeze until firm, about 2 hours.

Package 18 meatballs in each of three 1-quart freezer containers or freezer bags. Label and freeze no longer than 2 months.

Make-Ahead/Meatballs

◀ Quick & Easy Spaghetti

1 pkg. (7 oz.) spaghetti
1 container frozen Make-Ahead Tomato Meat Sauce, right

Grated Parmesan cheese

4 to 6 servings

Prepare spaghetti as directed on package. Rinse and drain. Cover. Set aside. Remove frozen Make-Ahead Tomato Meat Sauce from container and place in 2-quart casserole. Cover. Microwave at High for 18 to 25 minutes, or until hot and bubbly, breaking apart as soon as possible and stirring 2 or 3 times. Place spaghetti on large serving platter. Spoon sauce over spaghetti. Sprinkle with Parmesan cheese.

Quick & Easy Spaghetti
Lettuce Wedges with Italian Dressing   Garlic Toast   Chocolate Cake

◀ Old-Fashioned Goulash

1 cup uncooked elbow macaroni
1 container frozen Make-Ahead Tomato Meat Sauce, defrosted, right
1 can (8 oz.) whole kernel corn, drained
1 can (4 oz.) sliced mushrooms, drained

4 to 6 servings

Prepare macaroni as directed on package. Rinse and drain. In 2-quart casserole, combine macaroni, defrosted Make-Ahead Tomato Meat Sauce, corn and mushrooms. Mix well. Cover. Microwave at High for 8 to 14 minutes, or until hot, stirring twice.

Old-Fashioned Goulash
Leaf Lettuce & Sliced Carrot Salad   Frosted Cupcakes

◀ Spicy Chili

2 cups tomato juice
1 can (4 oz.) chopped green chilies, drained
1 tablespoon chili powder
¼ to ½ teaspoon ground cumin
⅛ teaspoon cayenne
1 container frozen Make-Ahead Tomato Meat Sauce, right
1 can (15½ oz.) kidney beans, drained

4 to 6 servings

In 2-quart casserole, combine tomato juice, chilies, chili powder, cumin and cayenne. Mix well. Cover. Microwave at High for 5 minutes. Add frozen Make-Ahead Tomato Meat Sauce. Re-cover. Microwave at High for 12 to 18 minutes, or until meat sauce is defrosted, breaking apart as soon as possible and stirring twice. Stir in beans. Re-cover. Microwave at High for 8 to 11 minutes, or until hot and bubbly. Top each serving with shredded Cheddar cheese, if desired.

Spicy Chili
Whole Grain Muffins   Lemon Sherbet

Make-Ahead Tomato Meat Sauce

1 lb. ground beef
¾ lb. bulk mild pork sausage
1 cup chopped onion
½ cup chopped celery
¼ cup finely chopped green pepper
1 clove garlic, minced
1 can (28 oz.) whole tomatoes, cut up
1 can (15 oz.) tomato sauce
1 can (6 oz.) tomato paste
1 tablespoon packed brown sugar
1 teaspoon salt
¾ teaspoon dried basil leaves
½ teaspoon dried marjoram leaves
¼ teaspoon pepper

2 containers
About 4 cups each

In 3-quart casserole, crumble beef and sausage. Stir in onion, celery, green pepper and garlic. Cover with wax paper. Microwave at High for 8 to 12 minutes, or until meat is no longer pink, stirring twice to break apart. Drain.

Add remaining ingredients. Mix well. Re-cover. Microwave at High for 30 to 40 minutes, or until mixture thickens and flavors are blended, stirring 3 or 4 times. Cool slightly.

Spoon into each of two 1-quart freezer containers or freezer bags. Label and freeze no longer than 4 months.

To defrost: Remove frozen sauce from one container and place in 2-quart casserole. Cover. Microwave at High for 7 to 10 minutes, or until defrosted, breaking apart as soon as possible and stirring once. Let stand, covered, for 5 minutes.

Savory Pork & Vegetables

Saucy Fish Bake

Italian Chicken Breasts

- 2 bone-in whole chicken breasts (10 to 12 oz. each) split in half, skin removed
- 1 container frozen Make-Ahead Vegetable Tomato Sauce, defrosted, right
- ¼ teaspoon dried oregano leaves

4 servings

Place chicken breast halves in 9-inch square baking dish. Spoon defrosted Make-Ahead Vegetable Tomato Sauce over chicken. Sprinkle with oregano. Cover with wax paper. Microwave at High for 13 to 18 minutes, or until chicken near bone is no longer pink and juices run clear, rearranging chicken once. Let stand, covered, for 3 minutes.

Italian Chicken Breasts
Buttered Broccoli Spears   Cheesy Garlic Bread   Lemon Crisp Cookies

Savory Pork & Vegetables

- 1 container frozen Make-Ahead Vegetable Tomato Sauce, defrosted, right
- 2 cups cut-up cooked pork roast
- ¼ teaspoon dried crushed sage leaves
- ¼ teaspoon salt
- ⅛ teaspoon pepper

4 servings

In 1½-quart casserole, combine defrosted Make-Ahead Vegetable Tomato Sauce, pork, sage, salt and pepper. Mix well. Cover. Microwave at 50% (Medium) for 12 to 17 minutes, or until flavors are blended, stirring twice.

Savory Pork & Vegetables
White Rice
Apple Crisp

Saucy Fish Bake

- 1 lb. fish fillets, about ½ inch thick, cut into serving-size pieces
- 1 container frozen Make-Ahead Vegetable Tomato Sauce, defrosted, right
- 1 cup shredded Monterey Jack cheese

4 to 6 servings

Arrange fish pieces in 10-inch square casserole. Spoon defrosted Make-Ahead Vegetable Tomato Sauce over fish. Cover. Microwave at High for 6 to 9 minutes, or until fish flakes easily with fork, rearranging fish once. Sprinkle cheese over fish. Microwave, uncovered, at 70% (Medium High) for 2 to 3 minutes, or until cheese melts, rotating casserole once.

Saucy Fish Bake
Romaine & Cucumber Salad
French Bread
Blueberry Turnovers

Make-Ahead Vegetable Tomato Sauce

- 1 can (16 oz.) whole tomatoes
- 1 can (12 oz.) tomato paste
- 1 cup coarsely chopped zucchini
- 1 cup sliced carrots, ¼ inch thick
- ½ cup chopped celery
- ½ cup chopped green pepper
- ¼ cup sliced green onions
- 2 tablespoons snipped fresh parsley
- 1 tablespoon olive oil
- ¼ teaspoon salt
- ⅛ teaspoon pepper
- 1 bay leaf

2 containers
1¾ cups each

In 2-quart casserole, combine all ingredients, except bay leaf. Mix well. Add bay leaf. Cover with wax paper. Microwave at High for 30 to 35 minutes, or until carrots and zucchini are tender-crisp and flavors are blended, stirring twice.

Remove bay leaf. Cool slightly. Spoon into two 1-pint freezer containers or freezer bags. Label and freeze no longer than 3 months.

To defrost: Remove frozen sauce from one container and place in 1-quart casserole. Cover. Microwave at High for 4 to 5 minutes, or until defrosted, stirring once or twice to break apart. Let stand, covered, for 5 minutes.

Pork Stew with Beans

- 2 lbs. pork stew meat, cut into ¾-inch pieces
- 1 cup cubed rutabaga, ¾-inch cubes
- 1 cup sliced celery, ½ inch thick
- 1 cup sliced carrots, ¼ inch thick
- 1 can (10¾ oz.) condensed beefy mushroom soup
- 1 can (8 oz.) tomato sauce
- 1 teaspoon bouquet sauce
- 1 teaspoon dried parsley flakes
- ½ teaspoon dried thyme leaves
- ¼ teaspoon pepper
- 1 can (19 oz.) white kidney beans, drained

2 containers
4 servings each

In 3-quart casserole, combine all ingredients, except beans. Cover. Microwave at High for 10 minutes. Stir. Re-cover. Microwave at 50% (Medium) for 50 minutes to 1 hour, or until pork and rutabaga are tender, stirring once. Stir in beans. Cool slightly.

Spoon into two 1-quart freezer containers or freezer bags. Label and freeze no longer than 4 months.

To serve: Remove frozen stew from container and place in 1½-quart casserole. Cover. Microwave at High for 5 minutes. Microwave at 70% (Medium High) for 15 to 23 minutes, or until hot, breaking apart as soon as possible and stirring twice.

Pork Stew with Beans
Pear Halves on Lettuce
Chocolate Chip Cookies

Beef & Lentil Soup

- 1½ lbs. beef stew meat, cut into ½-inch pieces
- 1 can (16 oz.) stewed tomatoes
- 1 can (14½ oz.) ready-to-serve beef broth
- 1 cup water
- 1 cup coarsely chopped cabbage
- 1 medium onion, coarsely chopped
- ½ cup coarsely chopped green pepper
- ⅓ cup uncooked dried lentils
- 1 teaspoon salt
- ½ teaspoon dried marjoram leaves
- ⅛ teaspoon pepper

2 containers
4 servings each

In 3-quart casserole, combine all ingredients. Mix well. Cover. Microwave at High for 10 minutes. Stir. Re-cover. Microwave at 50% (Medium) for 50 minutes to 1 hour, or until beef is tender, stirring once. Cool slightly.

Spoon into two 1-quart freezer containers or freezer bags. Label and freeze no longer than 4 months.

To serve: Remove frozen soup from container and place in 1½-quart casserole. Cover. Microwave at High for 17 to 25 minutes, or until hot, breaking apart as soon as possible and stirring twice.

Beef & Lentil Soup
Biscuits
Apple Slices and Green Grapes

Curried Turkey & Rice

- 1½ lbs. turkey tenderloins, cut into 1-inch cubes
- 2⅔ cups hot water
- 1⅓ cups uncooked long grain rice
- ½ cup chopped red pepper
- ¼ cup orange juice
- 1 tablespoon butter or margarine
- 2 teaspoons instant minced onion
- 1½ teaspoons instant chicken bouillon granules
- 1 teaspoon curry powder
- ½ teaspoon salt
- 1 cup frozen peas

2 containers
4 servings each

In 3-quart casserole, combine all ingredients, except peas. Mix well. Cover. Microwave at High for 10 minutes. Stir. Re-cover. Microwave at 50% (Medium) for 35 to 45 minutes, or until liquid is absorbed and rice is tender, stirring twice. Stir in peas. Cool.

Spoon into two 1-quart freezer containers or freezer bags. Label and freeze no longer than 4 months.

To serve: Remove frozen turkey and rice mixture from container and place in 1½-quart casserole. Cover. Microwave at High for 5 minutes. Microwave at 70% (Medium High) for 15 to 22 minutes, or until hot, breaking apart as soon as possible and stirring twice. If necessary, stir in 2 tablespoons to ¼ cup hot water during last 5 minutes of cooking time.

Curried Turkey & Rice
Marinated Tomato Slices
Carrot Cake with
Cream Cheese Frosting

Turkey-filled Cabbage Rolls

- 1 medium head cabbage, about 2 lbs.
- 1 lb. ground turkey
- ¼ cup chopped onion
- ¾ cup cooked rice
- 1 egg, slightly beaten
- 1 teaspoon salt
- ¼ teaspoon dried thyme leaves
- ⅛ teaspoon pepper
- Dash ground allspice

4 servings

Turkey-filled Cabbage Rolls
White Rice
Whole Wheat Rolls
Melon Cubes, Blueberries & Mandarin Oranges with Honey Dressing

How to Microwave & Freeze Turkey-filled Cabbage Rolls

Remove core from cabbage. Rinse and shake out excess water. Wrap cabbage in plastic wrap. Microwave at High for 5 to 7 minutes, or until outer leaves soften. Let stand for 5 minutes. Carefully remove 8 outer leaves.

Cut hard center rib from bottom of each leaf. Place four leaves on plate. Cover with plastic wrap. Microwave at High for 1½ to 2 minutes, or until leaves are pliable. Repeat with remaining four leaves. Set aside.

Serving Directions for Turkey-filled Cabbage Rolls

4 servings:
- 2 cans (7¾ oz. each) semi-condensed tomato soup
- 2 tablespoons thinly sliced green onion
- 1 teaspoon lemon juice
- ¼ teaspoon dried thyme leaves
- 8 frozen cabbage rolls

In 10-inch square casserole, combine soup, onion, lemon juice and thyme. Mix well. Unwrap 8 frozen cabbage rolls and add to soup mixture. Spoon soup mixture over cabbage rolls. Cover. Microwave at High for 19 to 26 minutes, or until heated through, rearranging and spooning sauce over cabbage rolls once.

1 serving:
- 1 can (7¾ oz.) semi-condensed tomato soup
- 1 tablespoon thinly sliced green onion
- ½ teaspoon lemon juice
- ⅛ teaspoon dried thyme leaves
- 2 frozen cabbage rolls

In 1-quart casserole, combine soup, onion, lemon juice and thyme. Mix well. Unwrap 2 frozen cabbage rolls and add to soup mixture. Spoon soup mixture over cabbage rolls. Cover. Microwave at High for 10 to 13 minutes, or until heated through, rearranging and spooning sauce over cabbage rolls once.

Crumble turkey into 1½-quart casserole. Add onion. Cover. Microwave at High for 4 to 7 minutes, or until turkey is firm, stirring once or twice to break apart. Drain thoroughly.

Stir in remaining ingredients. Mix well. Place about ⅓ cup turkey mixture on each cabbage leaf. Fold edges over, completely enclosing filling. Place cabbage rolls on wax paper-lined tray. Freeze about 1 hour. Wrap each cabbage roll in plastic wrap.

Package 8 cabbage rolls in one 1-gallon freezer bag or 2 cabbage rolls in each of four 1-pint freezer bags. Label and freeze no longer than 3 months.

Cheese-filled Manicotti

- 16 uncooked manicotti shells
- 2 tablespoons sliced green onion
- 2 tablespoons snipped fresh parsley
- 1 clove garlic, minced
- 1 tablespoon olive oil
- ½ teaspoon Italian seasoning
- 1 carton (15 oz.) ricotta cheese
- 2 cups shredded mozzarella cheese
- ½ cup grated Parmesan cheese
- 2 eggs, slightly beaten
- ½ teaspoon salt
- ⅛ teaspoon pepper

8 servings

Cheese-filled Manicotti
Asparagus Spears with Sliced Almonds
Strawberry Sorbet & Sugar Cookies

How to Microwave & Freeze Cheese-filled Manicotti

Prepare manicotti shells as directed on package. Rinse and drain. Set aside.

Combine onion, parsley, garlic, olive oil and Italian seasoning in medium mixing bowl. Cover with plastic wrap. Microwave at High for 2 to 2½ minutes, or until onion is tender. Cool slightly.

Add ricotta, mozzarella and Parmesan cheeses, eggs, salt and pepper. Mix well. Stuff each manicotti shell with about ¼ cup cheese filling. Wrap each shell in plastic wrap.

Serving Directions for Cheese-filled Manicotti

4 servings:
- 8 frozen stuffed manicotti shells
- ¼ cup olive oil
- 2 tablespoons tomato paste
- 2 teaspoons parsley flakes
- ¼ teaspoon salt
- ¼ teaspoon dried basil leaves
- 1 cup seeded chopped tomato, drained

Unwrap frozen stuffed manicotti shells. Place on 12-inch platter. Cover with plastic wrap. Microwave at 70% (Medium High) for 13 to 16 minutes, or until hot, rearranging once. In small bowl, combine remaining ingredients, except tomato. Microwave at High for 1 to 2 minutes, or until hot. Stir in tomato. Microwave at High for 1 minute. Spoon tomato mixture over manicotti.

1 serving:
- 2 frozen stuffed manicotti shells
- 1 tablespoon olive oil
- 1½ teaspoons tomato paste
- 1 teaspoon parsley flakes
- Dash salt
- Dash dried basil leaves
- ¼ cup seeded chopped tomato, drained

Unwrap frozen stuffed manicotti shells and place on plate. Cover with plastic wrap. Microwave at 70% (Medium High) for 4 to 6 minutes, or until hot. In small bowl, combine remaining ingredients, except tomato. Microwave at High for 30 seconds, or until hot. Stir in tomato. Microwave at High for 1 minute. Spoon tomato mixture over manicotti.

Package 8 shells in each of two 1-gallon freezer bags or 2 shells in each of eight 1-pint size freezer bags. Label and freeze no longer than 1 month.

Make-Ahead/Batch Cooking

Index

A

Alfalfa Sprouts,
  Sprouts & Beef Pitas, 120
Apples,
  Chicken with Sausage & Apple Stuffing, 49
Apricot-glazed Turkey, 62
Apricots,
  Fruited Ham Slice, 42
  Fruited Pork Ragout, 95
Artichokes,
  Chicken & Linguine, 125
  Chicken Breasts with Artichoke Sauce, 101
Asparagus,
  Hot Rotini & Seafood Salad, 134

B

Bacon,
  Bacon Spaghetti Sauce, 122
  Beef Tenderloin with Carrots & Leeks, 90
  Broccoli-topped Turkey Patties, 129
  Chicken Tetrazzini, 58
  Creamy Clam Chowder, 79
  Easy Turkey Loaf, 66
  Refrigerator Storage Chart, 10
Barbecued Chicken Sandwich, 126
Barbecued Pork Slices, 40
Basque-style Turkey Tenderloins, 106
Beans,
  Beef-n-Beans, 32
  Easy Beans & Rice, 85
  How to Stock the Pantry, 8
  Meatball & Potato Dinner, 143
  One-Dish Chicken Teriyaki, 56
  Pork Stew with Beans, 149
  Quick Chicken & Rice, 54
  Red Beans with Rice, 85
  Spicy Chili, 145
  Tuna Pie, 75
Beef,
  also see: Ground Beef
  Beef & Lentil Soup, 149
  Beef Strips & Sour Cream Gravy, 24
  Beef Tenderloin with Carrots & Leeks, 90
  Burgundy Beef with Peppers, 91
  Creamy Cubed Steak Casserole, 22
  Creamy Rice & Beef Dinner, 36
  Defrosting, 16
  Deli Beef Rolls, 25
  Family Swiss Steak, 21
  Fast & Easy Beef Stew, 23
  Freezer, How to Stock the, 12
  Freezer Storage Chart, 13
  German Marinated Beef, 89
  Greek Kabobs, 117
  Refrigerator Storage Chart, 10
  Reuben Bake, 35
  Rosemary-Peppered Rib Roast, 89
  Salsa-marinated Ribs, 22
  Smoked Beef-stuffed Peppers, 37
  Sprouts & Beef Pitas, 120
  Tangy Round Steak, 21
  Warm Sirloin Salad, 117
Beef-n-Beans, 32
Beets,
  Warm Sirloin Salad, 117
Braised Pork Chops with Sweet Peppers, 94
Broccoli,
  Broccoli-topped Turkey Patties, 129
  Cheesy Broccoli-stuffed Meatloaf, 26
  Hot Tortellini Salad, 123
  Italian Chowder, 44
  Oyster-Broccoli Au Gratin, 78
  Sausage & Mushroom-Rice Bake, 45
  Shrimp & Broccoli Teriyaki, 133
Brussels Sprouts,
  Creamy Cubed Steak Casserole, 22
Bulgur,
  Chicken & Vegetables with Bulgur, 126
Burger & Creamy Noodles, 34
Burgundy Beef with Peppers, 91

C

Cabbage,
  Chops & Creamed Cabbage, 40
  Easy Sausage & Cabbage, 46
  Turkey-filled Cabbage Rolls, 150
Carrots,
  Beef Tenderloin with Carrots & Leeks, 90
  Chicken & Linguine, 125
  Pork Stew with Beans, 149
  Stock the Refrigerator, How to, 10
Casseroles,
  Burger & Creamy Noodles, 34
  Cheese Grits, 84
  Cheesy Mac & Burger, 32
  Cheesy Tuna Bake, 76
  Chicken & Spinach Rice, 59
  Confetti Ham Casserole, 43
  Creamy Cubed Steak Casserole, 22
  Creamy Rice & Beef Dinner, 36
  Curried Turkey & Rice, 149
  Deluxe Macaroni & Cheese, 83
  Easy Beans & Rice, 85
  Easy Sausage & Cabbage, 46
  Hearty Sausage & Potato Casserole, 46
  Individual Spinach Stratas, 81
  Mediterranean Layered Casserole, 30
  Old-Fashioned Goulash, 145
  Oyster-Broccoli Au Gratin, 78
  Reheat Casseroles, Soups, and Stews, How to, 11
  Reheating, About, 11
  Reuben Bake, 35
  Salmon-Noodle Casserole, 75
  Sausage & Mushroom-Rice Bake, 45
  Spanish Tuna Casserole, 76
  Speedy Burger & Rice, 34
  Spicy Shrimp Bake, 79
Cheese,
  Cheese-filled Manicotti, 152
  Cheese Grits, 84
  Cheesy Broccoli-stuffed Meatloaf, 26
  Cheesy Chicken Potato Topper, 127
  Cheesy Chili-stuffed Tortillas, 82
  Cheesy Mac & Burger, 32
  Cheesy Tuna Bake, 76
  Chicken Tetrazzini, 58
  Chicken with Mornay Sauce, 102
  Deluxe Macaroni & Cheese, 83
  Double Cheese Linguine, 84
  Fillets with Swiss Cheese Sauce, 70
  Individual Spinach Stratas, 81
  Italian Meatball Dinner, 29
  Meatballs & Mostaccioli, 143
  Oyster-Broccoli Au Gratin, 78
  Pepper & Mushroom Melt Burgers, 118
  Pizza Bake, 44
  Pork Enchiladas, 47
  Quick & Easy Chicken Cacciatore, 56
  Quick Mexican Fish Fillets, 73
  Quick Mexican Pizzas, 118
  Refrigerator, How to Stock the, 10
  Reuben Bake, 35
  Saucy Fish Bake, 147
  Spicy Shrimp Bake, 79
  Cheesy Broccoli-stuffed Meatloaf, 26
  Cheesy Chicken Potato Topper, 127
  Cheesy Chili-stuffed Tortillas, 82
  Cheesy Mac & Burger, 32
  Cheesy Tuna Bake, 76
Chicken,
  Barbecued Chicken Sandwich, 126
  Cheesy Chicken Potato Topper, 127
  Chicken & Linguine, 125
  Chicken & Pea Pod Medley, 130
  Chicken & Spinach Rice, 59
  Chicken & Vegetables with Bulgur, 126
  Chicken Breasts with Artichoke Sauce, 101
  Chicken in Spicy Peanut Sauce, 101
  Chicken Tetrazzini, 58
  Chicken with Mornay Sauce, 102
  Chicken with Sausage & Apple Stuffing, 49
  Chinese Chicken with Vegetables, 104

Country-style Chicken, 52
Creamy Chicken & Vegetables, 55
Defrosting, 15, 17
Easy Hungarian Chicken, 51
Easy Sweet & Sour Chicken, 61
Family Favorite Chicken, 50
Freezer Storage Chart, 13
Individual Chicken Stew with
  Dumplings, 60
Italian Chicken Breasts, 147
One-Dish Chicken Teriyaki, 56
Oriental Chicken & Vegetables, 57
Quick & Easy Chicken Cacciatore, 56
Quick Chicken & Rice, 54
Refrigerator Storage Chart, Poultry, 10
Spicy Chicken Curry, 103
Chili,
  Spicy Chili, 145
Chinese Chicken with Vegetables, 104
Chinese Chow Mein, 29
Chops,
  Defrosting, 15, 16
  Lamb,
    Freezer Storage Chart, 13
    Lamb Chops with Minty Pear
      Sauce, 97
    Refrigerator Storage Chart, 10
  Pork,
    Braised Pork Chops with Sweet
      Peppers, 94
    Freezer Storage Chart, 13
    Chops & Creamed Cabbage, 40
    Pork Chops with Whole Wheat-Prune
      Stuffing, 93
    Quick Creole Chops, 39
    Refrigerator Storage Chart, 10
  Chops & Creamed Cabbage, 40
Chorizo Sausage Tacos, 121
Chowders,
  Creamy Clam Chowder, 79
  Ham & Corn Chowder, 122
  Hearty Fish Chowder, 69
  Italian Chowder, 44
  Reheating, About, 11
  Reheat Casseroles, Soups, and
    Stews, How to, 11
  Salmon-Rice Chowder, 74
Clams,
  Creamy Clam Chowder, 79
Cod,
  Defrosting Fish & Shellfish, 16
  Hearty Fish Chowder, 69
Confetti Ham Casserole, 43
Cooked Meats, Cut-up,
  Defrosting, 16
  Freezer, How to Stock the, 12
  Freezer Storage Chart, 13
  Refrigerator Storage Chart, 10
Corn,
  Burger & Creamy Noodles, 34
  Ham & Corn Chowder, 122
  Meatball Soup, 143
  Old-Fashioned Goulash, 145
Corned Beef,
  Reuben Bake, 35
Cornish Hens,
  Defrosting, 17
  Freezer Storage Chart, 13

Herb-seasoned Cornish Hens, 61
  Refrigerator Storage Chart, Poultry, 10
Country-style Chicken, 52
Crab,
  Crab à la King, 77
  Crab & Spinach-stuffed Shells, 136
  Crab Soup, 137
Creamy Chicken & Vegetables, 55
Creamy Clam Chowder, 79
Creamy Cubed Steak Casserole, 22
Creamy Rice & Beef Dinner, 36
Creamy Turkey & Vegetables, 131
Creole-sauced Turkey, 64
Cubed Steak,
  Creamy Cubed Steak Casserole, 22
  Defrosting, 16
  Fast & Easy Beef Stew, 23
  Freezer Storage Chart, 13
  Refrigerator Storage Chart, 13
Curried Turkey & Rice, 149
Curry,
  Spicy Chicken Curry, 103

D

Deli Beef Rolls, 25
Deluxe Macaroni & Cheese, 83
Double Cheese Linguine, 84
Defrosting,
  About Defrosting, 15
  Defrosting Fish & Shellfish, 16
  Defrosting Meat, 16
  Defrosting Poultry, 17
  How to Defrost Chops or Pieces, 15
  How to Defrost Cubed or Ground
    Meats, 15

E

Easy Beans & Rice, 85
Easy Hungarian Chicken, 51
Easy Sausage & Cabbage, 46
Easy Sweet & Sour Chicken, 61
Easy Turkey Loaf, 66
Eggs,
  Individual Spinach Stratas, 81
  Refrigerator, How to Stock the, 10
  Refrigerator Storage Chart, 10
  Smoked Salmon Omelet, 139

F

Family Favorite Chicken, 50
Family Pleasin' Meatloaf, 25
Family Swiss Steak, 21
Fast & Easy Beef Stew, 23
Fillets with Buttery Filbert Sauce, 113
Fillets with Swiss Cheese Sauce, 70
Fish,
  also see: Seafood
  Cheesy Tuna Bake, 76
  Defrosting, 16
  Fillets with Buttery Filbert Sauce, 113

Fillets with Swiss Cheese Sauce, 70
Fish in Spicy Red Sauce, 72
Fish with Shrimp Sauce, 110
Freezer Storage Chart, 13
Grouper with Dijon Butter, 133
Hearty Fish Chowder, 69
Herb Buttered Fish Fillets, 69
How to Stock the Freezer, 12
Lemony Fillets & Rice, 71
Quick Mexican Fish Fillets, 73
Refrigerator Storage Chart, 10
Salmon-Noodle Casserole, 75
Salmon-Rice Chowder, 74
Salmon-Rice Salad, 138
Salmon Steaks with Peppers, 111
Saucy Fish Bake, 147
Smoked Salmon Omelet, 139
Sole with Spicy Vegetable Sauce, 112
Spanish Tuna Casserole, 76
Summer Tuna Platter, 135
Trout & Mushroom Sauce, 135
Tuna Pie, 75
Freezer,
  Fast & Easy from the Freezer, 12
  Freezer, How to Stock the, 12
  Freezer Management, 12
  Freezer Packaging, 14
  Freezer Storage Chart, 13
Fruited Ham Slice, 42
Fruited Pork Ragout, 95
Fruits,
  Basque-style Turkey Tenderloins, 106
  Chicken with Sausage & Apple
    Stuffing, 49
  Easy Sweet & Sour Chicken, 61
  Fruited Ham Slice, 42
  Fruited Pork Ragout, 95
  Hawaiian Patties, 42
  Hot Smoked Turkey Salad, 125
  Lamb Chops with Minty Pear
    Sauce, 97
  Pork Chops with Whole Wheat-Prune
    Stuffing, 93
  Turkey Cutlets with Gingered Peach
    Sauce, 107

G

Garbanzo Beans,
  Easy Beans & Rice, 85
German Marinated Beef, 89
Grains,
  Cheese Grits, 84
  Chicken & Vegetables with
    Bulgur, 126
Great Northern Beans,
  Easy Beans & Rice, 85
  Italian Chowder, 44
Greek Kabobs, 117
Green Beans,
  Meatball & Potato Dinner, 143
  One-Dish Chicken Teriyaki, 56
  Quick Chicken & Rice, 54
  Tuna Pie, 75
Grits,
  Cheese Grits, 84

155

Ground Beef,
  Beef-n-Beans, 32
  Burger & Creamy Noodles, 34
  Cheesy Broccoli-stuffed Meatloaf, 26
  Cheesy Mac & Burger, 32
  Chinese Chow Mein, 29
  Defrosting, 16
  Family Pleasin' Meatloaf, 25
  Freezer Storage Chart, 13
  Freezer, How to Stock the, 12
  Italian Meatball Dinner, 29
  Italian Soup, 117
  Make-Ahead Freezer Meatballs, 143
  Make-Ahead Tomato Meat Sauce, 145
  Meat & Potato Bake, 28
  Meatball & Potato Dinner, 143
  Meatball Soup, 143
  Meatballs & Mostaccioli, 143
  Mediterranean Layered Casserole, 30
  Old-Fashioned Goulash, 145
  Quick & Easy Spaghetti, 145
  Quick Mexican Pizzas, 118
  Refrigerator Storage Chart, 10
  Salisbury Steak with Mushroom Sauce, 28
  Southwestern Chili Pie, 33
  Speedy Burger & Rice, 34
  Spicy Chili, 145

Ground Lamb,
  Defrosting, 15, 16
  Freezer Storage Chart, 13
  Mediterranean Layered Casserole, 30
  Refrigerator Storage Chart, 10

Ground Pork,
  Defrosting, 15, 16
  Freezer Storage Chart, 13
  Pork Enchiladas, 47
  Refrigerator Storage Chart, 10

Ground Turkey,
  Broccoli-topped Turkey Patties, 129
  Defrosting, 15, 17
  Freezer, How to Stock the, 12
  Freezer Storage Chart, 13
  Easy Turkey Loaf, 66
  Home-style Turkey Hash, 67
  Refrigerator Storage Chart, 10
  Turkey-filled Cabbage Rolls, 151

Grouper,
  Grouper with Dijon Butter, 133

H

Ham,
  Confetti Ham Casserole, 43
  Defrosting Meats, 16
  Freezer Storage Chart, 13
  Fruited Ham Slice, 42
  Ham & Corn Chowder, 122
  Hawaiian Patties, 42
  Hot Tortellini Salad, 123
  Refrigerator Storage Chart, 10
Hawaiian Patties, 42
Hearty Fish Chowder, 69
Hearty Sausage & Potato Casserole, 46
Herb Buttered Fish Fillets, 69
Herb-seasoned Cornish Hens, 61
Home-style Turkey Hash, 67
Hot Rotini & Seafood Salad, 134
Hot Smoked Turkey Salad, 125
Hot Tortellini Salad, 123

How to,
  Defrost Chops or Pieces, 15
  Defrost Cubed or Ground Meat, 15
  Make a Tomato Garnish, 89
  Make an Orange Zest, 93
  Microwave & Freeze Cheese-filled Manicotti, 152
  Microwave & Freeze Turkey-filled Cabbage Rolls, 150
  Microwave Apricot-glazed Turkey, 62
  Microwave Braised Pork Chops with Sweet Peppers, 94
  Microwave Broccoli-topped Turkey Patties, 129
  Microwave Burgundy Beef with Peppers, 91
  Microwave Cheesy Broccoli-stuffed Meatloaf, 26
  Microwave Cheesy Chicken Potato Topper, 127
  Microwave Cheesy Chili-stuffed Tortillas, 82
  Microwave Chinese Chicken with Vegetables, 104
  Microwave Confetti Ham Casserole, 43
  Microwave Country-style Chicken, 52
  Microwave Crab & Spinach-stuffed Shells, 136
  Microwave Easy Turkey Loaf, 66
  Microwave Fillets with Buttery Filbert Sauce, 113
  Microwave Fish in Spicy Red Sauce, 72
  Microwave Hot Tortellini Salad, 123
  Microwave Individual Chicken Stew with Dumplings, 60
  Microwave Individual Spinach Stratas, 81
  Microwave Mediterranean Layered Casserole, 31
  Microwave Oriental Chicken & Vegetables, 57
  Microwave Oyster-Broccoli Au Gratin, 78
  Microwave Pepper & Mushroom Melt Burgers, 118
  Microwave Reuben Bake, 35
  Microwave Smoked Beef-stuffed Peppers, 37
  Microwave Smoked Salmon Omelet, 139
  Microwave Southwestern Chili Pie, 33
  Microwave Spicy Chicken Curry, 103
  Microwave Sprouts & Beef Pitas, 120
  Microwave Walnut-Tarragon Veal Cutlets, 98
  Package Cooked Foods, 14
  Reheat Casseroles, Soups and Stews, 11
  Reheat Combination Plates, 11
  Stock the Freezer, 13
  Stock the Pantry, 9
  Stock the Refrigerator, 10

I

Individual Chicken Stew with Dumplings, 60
Individual Spinach Stratas, 81
Italian Chicken Breasts, 147
Italian Chowder, 44
Italian Meatball Dinner, 29
Italian Soup, 117
Italian Turkey Cutlets, 106

K

Kabobs,
  Greek Kabobs, 117
Kidney Beans,
  Pork Stew with Beans, 149
  Red Beans with Rice, 85
  Spicy Chili, 145

L

Lamb,
  also see: Ground Lamb
  Defrosting Meats, 16
  Freezer Storage Chart, 13
  Lamb Chops with Minty Pear Sauce, 97
  Refrigerator Storage Chart, 10
  Summer Lamb Stew, 97
Leeks,
  Beef Tenderloin with Carrots & Leeks, 90
Lemony Fillets & Rice, 71
Lentils,
  Beef & Lentil Soup, 149

M

Make-Ahead Freezer Meatballs, 143
Make-Ahead Tomato Meat Sauce, 145
Make-Ahead Vegetable Tomato Sauce, 147
Meat & Potato Bake, 28
Meatball & Potato Dinner, 143
Meatball Soup, 143
Meatballs,
  Italian Meatball Dinner, 29
  Make-Ahead Freezer Meatballs, 143
  Meatball & Potato Dinner, 143
  Meatball Soup, 143
  Meatballs & Mostaccioli, 143
Meatless,
  Cheese-filled Manicotti, 152
  Cheese Grits, 84
  Cheesy Chili-stuffed Tortillas, 82
  Deluxe Mcaroni & Cheese, 83
  Double Cheese Linguine, 84
  Easy Beans & Rice, 85
  Individual Spinach Stratas, 81
  Red Beans with Rice, 85

Meatloaf,
  Cheesy Broccoli-stuffed Meatloaf, 26
  Family Pleasin' Meatloaf, 25
  Meat & Potato Bake, 28
Mediterranean Layered Casserole, 30
Mostaccioli,
  Meatballs and Mostaccioli, 143
Mushrooms,
  Burgundy Beef with Peppers, 91
  Chicken & Linguine, 125
  Mushroom Sauce, 28
  Saucy Veal & Mushrooms, 99
  Sausage & Mushroom-Rice Bake, 45
  Shrimp & Broccoli Teriyaki, 133
  Szechwan Shrimp, 110
  Trout & Mushroom Sauce, 135
Mussels,
  Shellfish Dinner for Two, 109
Mustard Turkey Slices, 65

N

Nuts,
  Fillets with Buttery Filbert Sauce, 113
  Pantry, How to Stock the, 9
  Walnut-Tarragon Veal Cutlets, 98

O

Old-Fashioned Goulash, 145
One-Dish Chicken Teriyaki, 56
Orange Roughy,
  Fillets with Buttery Filbert Sauce, 113
Oranges,
  Easy Sweet & Sour Chicken, 61
  Hot Smoked Turkey Salad, 125
  Salmon-Rice Salad, 138
Oriental Chicken & Vegetables, 57
Oysters,
  Oyster-Broccoli Au Gratin, 78

P

Packaging,
  Freezer Packaging, 14
  Package Cooked Foods, How to, 14
  Packaging Cooked Foods, 14
Pantry,
  Pantry, How to Stock the, 9
  What to Keep on Hand In Your Pantry, 8
Pasta,
  Burger & Creamy Noodles, 34
  Cheese-filled Manicotti, 152
  Cheesy Mac & Burger, 32
  Chicken & Linguine, 125
  Chicken Tetrazzini, 58
  Confetti Ham Casserole, 43
  Crab & Spinach-stuffed Shells, 136
  Creamy Turkey & Vegetables, 131
  Deluxe Macaroni & Cheese, 83
  Double Cheese Linguine, 84

  Easy Hungarian Chicken, 51
  Hot Rotini & Seafood Salad, 134
  Hot Smoked Turkey Salad, 125
  Hot Tortellini Salad, 123
  Italian Chowder, 44
  Italian Soup, 117
  Old-Fashioned Goulash, 145
  Pantry, How to Stock the, 9
  Pizza Bake, 44
  Quick & Easy Spaghetti, 145
  Reuben Bake, 35
  Salmon-Noodle Casserole, 75
Pea Pods
  Chicken & Pea Pod Medley, 130
Peaches,
  Turkey Cutlets with Gingered Peach Sauce, 107
Pears,
  Lamb Chops with Minty Pear Sauce, 97
Peas,
  Curried Turkey & Rice, 149
  Double Cheese Linguine, 84
  Speedy Burger & Rice, 34
Peas and Carrots,
  Creamy Rice & Beef Dinner, 36
  Salmon-Rice Chowder, 74
Pepper & Mushroom Melt Burgers, 118
Peppers,
  Braised Pork Chops with Sweet Peppers, 94
  Burgundy Beef with Peppers, 91
  Salmon Steaks with Peppers, 111
  Smoked Beef-stuffed Peppers, 37
Pies,
  Southwestern Chili Pie, 33
  Tuna Pie, 75
Pineapple,
  Easy Sweet & Sour Chicken, 61
  Fruited Ham Slice, 42
  Hawaiian Patties, 42
Pizza Bake, 44
Pork,
  also see: Ground Pork
  Bacon Spaghetti Sauce, 122
  Barbecued Pork Slices, 40
  Braised Pork Chops with Sweet Peppers, 94
  Broccoli-topped Turkey Patties, 129
  Chicken with Sausage & Apple Stuffing, 49
  Chops & Creamed Cabbage, 40
  Chorizo Sausage Tacos, 121
  Confetti Ham Casserole, 43
  Defrosting, 15, 16
  Easy Sausage & Cabbage, 46
  Freezer, How to Stock the, 12
  Freezer Storage Chart, 13
  Fruited Ham Slice, 42
  Fruited Pork Ragout, 95
  Ham & Corn Chowder, 122
  Hawaiian Patties, 42
  Hearty Sausage & Potato Casserole, 46
  Hot Tortellini Salad, 123
  Italian Chowder, 44
  Make-Ahead Tomato Meat Sauce, 145
  Pizza Bake, 44

  Pork Chops with Whole Wheat-Prune Stuffing, 93
  Pork Enchiladas, 47
  Pork Medallions in Cream Sauce, 93
  Pork Stew with Beans, 149
  Quick Creole Chops, 39
  Refrigerator Storage Chart, 10
  Sausage & Mushroom-Rice Bake, 45
  Savory Pork & Vegetables, 147
  Teriyaki Orange Ribs, 41
Potatoes,
  Cheesy Chicken Potato Topper, 127
  Country-style Chicken, 52
  Crab Soup, 137
  Creamy Cubed Steak Casserole, 22
  Ham & Corn Chowder, 122
  Hearty Sausage & Potato Casserole, 46
  Home-style Turkey Hash, 67
  Meat & Potato Bake, 28
  Meatball & Potato Dinner, 143
  Mediterranean Layered Casserole, 301
  Summer Tuna Platter, 135
Poultry,
  Apricot-glazed Turkey, 62
  Barbecued Chicken Sandwich, 126
  Basque-style Turkey Tenderloins, 106
  Brocolli-topped Turkey Patties, 129
  Cheesy Chicken Potato Topper, 127
  Chicken & Linguine, 125
  Chicken & Pea Pod Medley, 130
  Chicken & Spinach Rice, 59
  Chicken & Vegetables with Bulgur, 126
  Chicken Breasts with Artichoke Sauce, 101
  Chicken in Spicy Peanut Sauce, 101
  Chicken Tetrazzini, 58
  Chicken with Mornay Sauce, 102
  Chicken with Sausage & Apple Stuffing, 49
  Chinese Chicken with Vegetables, 104
  Country-style Chicken, 52
  Creamy Chicken & Vegetables, 55
  Creamy Turkey & Vegetables, 131
  Creole-sauced Turkey, 64
  Curried Turkey & Rice, 149
  Defrosting, 17
  Easy Hungarian Chicken, 51
  Easy Sweet & Sour Chicken, 61
  Easy Turkey Loaf, 66
  Family Favorite Chicken, 50
  Freezer, How to Stock the, 12
  Freezer Storage Chart, 13
  Herb-seasoned Cornish Hens, 61
  Home-style Turkey Hash, 67
  Hot Smoked Turkey Salad, 125
  Individual Chicken Stew with Dumplings, 60
  Italian Chicken Breasts, 147
  Italian Turkey Cutlets, 106
  Mustard Turkey Slices, 65
  One-Dish Chicken Teriyaki, 56
  Oriental Chicken & Vegetables, 57
  Quick & Easy Chicken Cacciatore, 56
  Quick Chicken & Rice, 54
  Refrigerator Storage Chart, 10

Savory Italian Turkey, 63
Spicy Chicken Curry, 103
Turkey & Leek Soup, 131
Turkey Cutlets with Gingered Peach Sauce, 107
Turkey-filled Cabbage Rolls, 150
Prunes,
  Pork Chops with Whole Wheat-Prune Stuffing, 93

Q

Quick & Easy Chicken Cacciatore, 56
Quick & Easy Spaghetti, 145
Quick Chicken & Rice, 54
Quick Creole Chops, 39
Quick Mexican Fish Fillets, 73
Quick Mexican Pizzas, 118

R

Red Beans with Rice, 85
Refrigerator,
  Refrigerator, How to Stock the, 10
  Refrigerator Management, 10
  Refrigerator Storage Chart, 10
Reheating,
  Reheat Casseroles, Soups, and Stews, How to, 11
  Reheat Combination Plates, How to, 11
  Reheating, About, 11
Reuben Bake, 35
Ribs,
  Beef,
    Freezer Storage Chart, 13
    Refrigerator Storage Chart, 10
    Salsa Marinated Ribs, 22
  Defrosting, 15, 16
  Pork,
    Freezer Storage Chart, 13
    Refrigerator Storage Chart, 10
    Teriyaki Orange Ribs, 41
Rice,
  Chicken & Pea Pod Medley, 130
  Chicken & Spinach Rice, 59
  Creamy Rice & Beef Dinner, 36
  Curried Turkey & Rice, 149
  Easy Beans & Rice, 85
  Easy Sausage & Cabbage, 46
  Lemony Fillets & Rice, 71
  One-Dish Chicken Teriyaki, 56
  Quick Chicken & Rice, 54
  Salmon-Rice Chowder, 74
  Salmon-Rice Salad, 138
  Sausage & Mushroom-Rice Bake, 45
  Smoked Beef-stuffed Peppers, 37
  Southwestern Chili Pie, 33
  Spanish Tuna Casserole, 76
  Speedy Burger & Rice, 34
  Spicy Shrimp Bake, 79
  Tuna Pie, 75
Roasts,
  Beef,
    Defrosting, 16
    Freezer Storage Chart, 13

    Refrigerator Storage Chart, 10
    Rosemary Peppered Rib Roast, 89
  Rosemary-Peppered Rib Roast, 89
Round Steak
  Defrosting, 16
  Family Swiss Steak, 22
  Freezer Storage Chart, 13
  German Marinated Beef, 89
  Refrigerator Storage Chart, 10
  Saucy Veal & Mushrooms, 99
  Tangy Round Steak, 21
Rutabagas,
  Pork Stew with Beans, 149

S

Salads,
  Hot Rotini & Seafood Salad, 134
  Hot Smoked Turkey Salad, 125
  Hot Tortellini Salad, 123
  Salmon-Rice Salad, 138
  Summer Tuna Platter, 135
  Warm Sirloin Salad, 117
Salisbury Steak with Mushroom Sauce, 28
Salmon,
  Defrosting, 16
  Freezer Storage Chart, 13
  Refrigerator Storage Chart, 10
  Salmon-Noodle Casserole, 75
  Salmon-Rice Chowder, 74
  Salmon-Rice Salad, 138
  Salmon Steaks with Peppers, 111
  Smoked Salmon Omelet, 139
  Steaks, 16
Salsa-marinated Ribs, 22
Sandwiches,
  Barbecued Chicken Sandwich, 126
  Chorizo Sausage Tacos, 121
  Pepper & Mushroom Melt Burgers, 118
  Quick Mexican Pizzas, 118
  Sprouts & Beef Pitas, 120
Sauces,
  Bacon Spaghetti Sauce, 122
  Make-Ahead Tomato Meat Sauce, 145
  Make-Ahead Vegetable Tomato Sauce, 147
  Mushroom Sauce, 28
  Saucy Fish Bake, 147
  Saucy Veal & Mushrooms, 99
  Sauerkraut,
    Reuben Bake, 35
Sausage,
  Chicken with Sausage & Apple Stuffing, 49
  Chorizo Sausage Tacos, 121
  Easy Sausage & Cabbage, 46
  Freezer Storage Chart, 13
  Hearty Sausage & Potato Casserole, 46
  Italian Chowder, 44
  Make-Ahead Tomato Meat Sauce, 145
  Pizza Bake, 44
  Sausage & Mushroom-Rice Bake, 45
  Savory Italian Turkey, 63
  Savory Pork & Vegetables, 147

Scallops,
  Defrosting, 16
  Scallops with Coriander-Orange Sauce, 109
Seafood,
  Cheesy Tuna Bake, 76
  Crab à la King, 77
  Crab & Spinach-stuffed Shells, 136
  Crab Soup, 137
  Creamy Clam Chowder, 79
  Defrosting, 16
  Freezer, How to Stock the, 12
  Freezer Storage Chart, 13
  Fillets with Buttery Filbert Sauce, 113
  Fillets with Swiss Cheese Sauce, 70
  Fish in Shrimp Sauce, 110
  Fish in Spicy Red Sauce, 72
  Grouper with Dijon Butter, 133
  Hearty Fish Chowder, 69
  Herb Buttered Fish Fillets, 69
  Hot Rotini & Seafood Salad, 134
  Lemony Fillets & Rice, 71
  Oyster-Broccoli Au Gratin, 78
  Quick Mexican Fish Fillets, 73
  Refrigerator Storage Chart, 10
  Salmon-Noodle Casserole, 75
  Salmon-Rice Chowder, 74
  Salmon-Rice Salad, 138
  Salmon Steaks with Peppers, 111
  Saucy Fish Bake, 147
  Scallops with Coriander-Orange Sauce, 109
  Shellfish Dinner for Two, 109
  Shrimp & Broccoli Teriyaki, 133
  Smoked Salmon Omelet, 139
  Sole with Spicy Vegetable Sauce, 112
  Spanish Tuna Casserole, 76
  Spicy Shrimp Bake, 79
  Summer Tuna Platter, 135
  Szechwan Shrimp, 110
  Trout & Mushroom Sauce, 135
  Tuna Pie, 75
Shellfish Dinner for Two, 109
Shrimp,
  Defrosting, 16
  Fish with Shrimp Sauce, 110
  Freezer, How to Stock the, 12
  Freezer Storage Chart, 13
  Hot Rotini & Seafood Salad, 134
  Refrigerator Storage Chart, 10
  Shellfish Dinner for Two, 109
  Shrimp & Broccoli Teriyaki, 133
  Spicy Shrimp Bake, 79
  Szechwan Shrimp, 110
Smoked Beef-stuffed Peppers, 37
Smoked Salmon Omelet, 139
Sole,
  Defrosting, 16
  Freezer Storage Chart, 13
  Refrigerator Storage Chart, 10
  Sole with Spicy Vegetable Sauce, 112
Soups,
  Beef & Lentil Soup, 149
  Crab Soup, 137
  Italian Soup, 117
  Meatball Soup, 143
  Reheat Casseroles, Soups and Stews, How to, 11